P9-ARF-022

QUEEN ANNE'S
AMERICAN KINGS

Oxford University Press, Amen House, London E.C.4

GLASGOW NEW YORK TORONTO MELBOURNE WELLINGTON
BOMBAY CALCUTTA MADRAS CAPE TOWN

Geoffrey Cumberlege, Publisher to the University

・ THE FOUR INDIAN KINGS

Painted by Bernard Lens the Younger
Engraved by Bernard Lens the Elder

QUEEN ANNE'S
AMERICAN KINGS

By

RICHMOND P. BOND

OCTAGON BOOKS

A DIVISION OF FARRAR, STRAUS AND GIROUX

New York   1974

Behold, four Kings in majesty rever'd.

THE RAPE OF THE LOCK

Originally published in 1952 by the Clarendon Press

Reprinted 1974
by special arrangement with Oxford University Press, Inc.

OCTAGON BOOKS

A DIVISION OF FARRAR, STRAUS & GIROUX, INC.
19 Union Square West
New York, N. Y. 10003

LIBRARY OF CONGRESS CATALOG CARD NUMBER: 73-21361
ISBN 0-374-90783-8

Printed in U.S.A. by
NOBLE OFFSET PRINTERS, INC.
New York, N.Y. 10003

Preface

QUEEN ANNE'S American Kings were Iroquois sachems from the province of New York, escorted to London in 1710 in order to impress England with the urgency of Indian affairs and to be impressed by the power and grandeur of their step-mother country. The year before their visit the northern English-American colonists had known a large and expensive calamity when the Crown judged it necessary to abandon an expedition intended for the investment of Canada and the destruction of the French, long their rivals in arms, faith, and trade. Now, if the Indians would remain constant to the New Yorkers and New Englanders and if England would send against New France but a fraction of the strength she had directed against Old France, victory would be full and final. Resolved on a renewal of the expedition, colonial leaders decided to present their case at court, and to include in this diplomatic mission Iroquois sachems from the valley of the Mohawk who would serve as native ministers to sue for war and men and men-of-war, and would on return induce a stronger regard for England among their Confederacy. Guided by Colonels Francis Nicholson and Peter Schuyler, these Indian chiefs became in London a thrice-nine-days' wonder of the Town.

This volume about their visit is the end of a diversion undertaken for personal amusement and relief from the chores of Academe and the doubts of war and peace, and pursued in the notion that the enjoyment a man may have of his main road can be enlarged by an excursion into a by-way. The trail started with the fiftieth essay of the *Spectator*, and the sport lay in remarking how what would lead where. The visit of the sachems as an Anglo-

American-Indian episode is known to the reader of colonial and late Stuart history, wherein it generally receives a brief and derivative account; but the facts of and behind the visit, its ramification into church- and statecraft, and its connexion with art and letters are best discovered in such contemporary chronicles as the official records, annals and memoirs, published and unpublished correspondence, and 'the light squadrons of occasional pamphlets and flying sheets'. Upon such remains most of the following pages depend.

The princes from the West invaded more than public and private archives or ephemeral tracts and broadsides or the sheets of mere intelligence foreign and domestic. Daniel Defoe referred to them in his wide *Review of the State of the British Nation*; Alexander Pope suggested them, presumably, in *Windsor-Forest*; Dick Steele chose the visitors as topic for a *Tatler* paper; and Mr. Addison gave them a speculation in the *Spectator*. These men of letters were all in or near London during the visit of the Indian envoys and could have seen them at playhouse or in thoroughfare. Of the master craftsmen who gave fame to the reign of Anna Augusta only Jonathan Swift was too much removed to see the sachems, being himself in Ireland preparing for his campaign among the political placemen of England. Yet it was he who proposed to write the most extensive appearance of these Iroquois in English literature. A year after the Kings toured London, Swift, in a final instalment to a semi-monthly budget of news and views for Stella, commented on the *Spectator* of the day before, which he said was made of a hint he had once given the editor about the supposed travels of an Indian into England, and then added: 'I repent he ever had it. I intended to have written a book on that subject.'

A book on that subject is now perforce intended only as the history of an international interlude—a tale of New York and New England and New France, of the first

Mayor of Albany and the first Governor of Nova Scotia, of the Archbishop of Canterbury resting from his gout and the Reverend Mr. Andrews sleeping on a bear's skin, of the Society of Jesus and that for the Propagation of the Gospel in Foreign Parts, of Macbeth and Powell's puppets, of good prose and bad verse, of ships that sailed or not, and of one English Queen and her four American Kings.

R. P. B.

Contents

List of Plates

I

The Visit

ON the 19th day of April 1710, in the ninth year of the reign of Her Sacred Majesty Queen Anne, her people of London watched two of her coaches rolling through the streets on their way to St. James's Palace. In this royal progress Sir Charles Cotterell, as Master of Ceremonies, conducted four Indian sachems—'Kings' in England—to have audience of their Queen. Iroquois they were, named Te Yee Neen Ho Ga Prow, Sa Ga Yean Qua Prah Ton, Oh Nee Yeath Ton No Prow, and Elow Oh Kaom. With them rode Colonel Francis Nicholson, Colonel Peter Schuyler, Major David Pigeon, and Captain Abraham Schuyler.

The Kings, who were introduced into the royal presence by the Duke of Shrewsbury in one of his first duties as the new Lord Chamberlain, made a speech through their interpreter, Captain Schuyler, which Major Pigeon read in English to Her Majesty. 'We have undertaken a long and tedious Voyage, which none of our Predecessors could ever be prevail'd upon to undertake. The Motive that induc'd us was, that we might see our GREAT QUEEN, and relate to Her those things we thought absolutely necessary for the Good of HER and us Her Allies, on the other side the Great Water.' They go on to remind Anne how in the late lamented campaign against the French the Indians had put away the kettle and taken up the hatchet, but how the expected aid from England had not arrived. The reduction of Canada is so needful for their free hunting and great trade with the English, the sachems continue, that 'in Case our *Great Queen* should not be mindful of us, we must, with our Families, forsake our Country and seek other Habitations, or stand Neuter;

either of which will be much against our Inclinations'. They conclude with a request for missionaries, and present the Queen belts of wampum.

Her Majesty graciously accepted the address, ordered gifts for the visitors, and commanded that the Lord Chamberlain entertain them at her charge during their stay and that they be shown the city. After their audience the Kings were conducted back to their apartments at the 'Two Crowns and Cushions' in King Street. This 'very considerable and pleasant' way was hard by St. Paul's Church and led from the west into the spacious Covent Garden Square, which from the east received Russell Street, containing Will's Coffee-house, seat of the wits and Mr. Bickerstaff's poetical accounts. The sachems' host was an upholsterer, Thomas Arne, father of a month-old son who would make the music for 'Rule, Britannia', and later of a daughter who became the singing actress and wife to Theophilus Cibber, son of the Laureate.

Describing the Indian Kings, a current pamphleteer wrote with what may well have been eyewitness knowledge:

As to the Persons of these Princes, they are well form'd, being of a Stature neither too high nor too low, but all within an Inch or two of six Foot; their Habits are robust, and their Limbs muscular and well shap'd; they are of brown Complexions, their Hair black and long, their Visages are very awful and majestick, and their Features regular enough, though something of the austere and sullen; and the Marks with which they disfigure their Faces, do not seem to carry so much Terror as Regard with them. The Garments they wear, are black Wastcoats, Breeches, and Stockings, with yellow Slippers, and a loose scarlet mantle cast over them, bound with a Gold Gallon; their hair ty'd short up, and a Cap something of the Nature of a Turbant upon their heads. They are generally affable to all that come to see them, and will not refuse a Glass of Brandy or strong Liquors from any hands that offer it. They never sit on Chairs or Benches, but on their Heels, which makes their Knees, when they stand upright, bag out before. They feed heartily, and love our *English* Beef before all other Victuals that are provided for 'em; of which they have Variety at the Charge of the Publick, with the best of Wines; but they seem to relish our fine pale Ales before the best *French* Wines from *Burgundy* or *Champaign*.

Once the royal audience was over, the Kings entered a strenuous round of official events, a bewildering grand tour of London, and were themselves a spectacle to the city's mobile populace. On Thursday 20 April the Duke of Ormonde nobly treated them at dinner at his country seat near Richmond, and the next day they went in one of the Queen's barges to Greenwich, where they saw the house and mathematical instruments of Dr. Flamsteed, Astronomer Royal, and viewed Greenwich Hospital and the dock and yard at Woolwich, 'after which they were nobly treated by some of the Lords Commissioners of the Admiralty, in One of Her Majesty's Yatchs'. On the day following, according to Narcissus Luttrell, that indispensable annotator of book, battle, or anything, the sachems 'saw the banquetting house and chappel at Whitehal, and mightily pleased with their kind reception'. About this time one of the Kings fell ill and was forced the while to rest at the 'Two Crowns and Cushions'.

By then the sachems were a sensation, and one theatrical manager was quick to see that here might be a way to attract a large audience—perhaps fill the house. On 20 April the *Daily Courant* (then the sole diurnal paper) announced that on Monday next, 24 April, at the Queen's Theatre in the Haymarket, Congreve's *Old Bachelor* would be performed 'For the Entertainment of the Four INDIAN KINGS lately arriv'd', as a benefit for the actor William Bowen and with Mr. Betterton, no less, as the Bachelor. On the following day, however, probably because of Betterton's ill health, the play was changed to *Macbeth* with Mr. Wilks in the title role. Trinculo had said, 'When they will not give a doit to relieve a lame beggar, they will lay out ten to see a dead Indian', and here at the Haymarket would be four Indians alive, and Kings at that. On the 24th the Kings, but only three of them, went to the theatre and thus entered its history:

the curtain was drawn, but in vain did the players attempt to perform—the Mob, who had possession of the upper gallery, declared that they came to see the Kings, 'and since we have paid our money, the Kings we will have'—whereupon Wilks came forth, and assured them the Kings were in the front box —to this the Mob replied, they could not see them, and desired they might be placed in a more conspicuous point of view— 'otherwise there shall be no play'—Wilks assured them he had nothing so much at heart as their happiness, and accordingly got four chairs, and placed the Kings on the stage, to the no small satisfaction of the Mob, with whom it is a maxim to have as much as possible for their money.

A special epilogue had been written 'To be Spoken Before the Four Indian Kings, at the QUEEN's Theatre' on this occasion.

As *Sheba*'s Queen with Adoration came,
To pay Her Homage to a greater Name,
And struck with Wonder at the Monarch's Sight,
Thought the whole Globe, of Earth that Prince's Right.
Since Fame had fall'n much short in it's Report,
Of so renown'd a King, and so enrich'd a Court.
So now Great *Anna*'s most Auspicious Reign,
Not only makes one Soveraign cross the Main;
One Prince from Lands remote a Visit pay,
And come, and see, and wonder, and obey:
But wing'd by Her Example urges Four,
To seek Protection on *Britannia's* Shore.

The lines limp forward to call the attention of the monarchs to the encircling belles and beaux, the citizens and their wives, and to render the gratitude of the bene- fited Bowen.

At PUNCHs Theatre.

For the Entertainment of the

Four Indian Kings, viz.

- (A) The Emperor *Tee Yee Neen Ho Ga Row*.
- (B) King *Sa Ga Yean Qua Rab Tow*.
- (C) King *E Tow oh Koam*.
- (D) King *Ob Nee Yeath Tow no Riow*

This prefent Munday, May 1. at Seven a-Clock.

T the Upper End of St. *Martin's-Lane*, joyning to *Litchfield-ftreet*, will be Prefented a *NEW OPERA*, Performed by a Company of *Artificial Actors*, who will *prefent you* with an *incomparable Entertainment*, call'd,

The Laft Years CAMPAIGNE.

With the Famous Battle fought between the Confederate Army (Commanded by the Duke of *Marlborough*) and the *French* in the *Woods* near *Blaguiers*. With *feveral Comical Entertainments* of Punch *in the* Camp. Alfo *variety of Scenes*; with a *moft Glorious Profpect of both Armies, the French in their Entrenchments and the Confederates out; where will be feen feveral Regiments of Horfe and Foot Engaged in Forcing the* French Lines. *With the Admirable Entertainments of a Girl of Five Years old Dancing with Swords.* Note; *This Play will continue all the Week.* Box 2 *s.* Pit 1 *s.* Gallery 6 *d.*

Playbill of Performance of Powell's Puppets for the Entertainment of the Four Indian Kings

What the Iroquois thought of all this, of the audience, of Mr. Wilks's performance, of the aerial witches in Davenant's version of the play, of Shakespeare in general, and the Haymarket in particular, or how they described the scene to their ailing colleague—this there is of course no way to know. What the people of the theatre thought is clear—the Kings had proved to be a hit, and for the remainder of the week the Haymarket tagged all its performances 'For the Entertainment of the Four INDIAN KINGS', including ·*Hamlet*, Otway, two operas, and a one-act farce.

The Theatre Royal in Drury Lane quickly made its rival bid for profit by announcing two plays for the Kings. And for this royalty 'lately arriv'd in this Kingdom' 'At the Cockpit Royal in Cartwright street . . . this present Saturday the 29th of April, will be seen the Royal Sport of Cock-fighting for 2 Guineas a Battle, a Pair of Shagbags fight for 5 l. and a Battle Royal. Beginning exactly at 4 a Clock'. The *Tatler* as well as the *Courant* carried the advice that 'At the Desire of several Ladies of Quality, and for the Entertainment of the Emperor of the Mohocks, and the 3 Indian Kings, (being the last Time of their Appearance in Publick)' a 'Consort of Vocal and Instrumental Musick' would be given by Mrs. Hemmings and others for her benefit at the Great Room in York Buildings at eight on the following Monday, 1 May, it being the first time of her appearance in public, with tickets at five shillings. On the same day Powell the puppeteer offered the Kings at Punch's Theatre a new and most appropriate opera, *The Last Years Campaigne*, as 'Performed by a Company of *Artificial Actors*', augmented by a 'Girl of Five Years old Dancing with Swords'. Powell's handbill for the day was decorated with the crude figures of four swarthy crowned potentates who bore the names of the Indian Kings, to prove it all. And for Wednesday the 3rd of May, there was advertised in their honour 'A Tryal of

Skill to be fought at the Bear-Garden in Hockley in the Hole . . . between John Parkes from Coventry, and Thomas Hesgate a Barkshire-Man, at, these following Weapons, viz. Back-Sword, Sword and Dagger, Sword and Buckler, Single Falchon, Case of Falchons, and Quarter-Staff'.

Consider the sachems curiously following such a round of English amusement, the plays and assorted divertissements. Did they attempt to divide an evening between conflicting invitations to the Haymarket and Drury Lane, nearly equidistant in opposite directions from their lodgings, and between the simultaneous attractions of Mrs. Hemmings and Powell's puppets? Did they debate the merits of the fighting cocks, and decide for the sword play of, say, the man from Coventry? There is assurance only that, of tragedy, comedy, farce, opera, concert, puppet show, cock-fight, and trial of skill at swords announced in their name, the Kings saw Mr. Wilks as Macbeth, King of Scotland.

But certain it is that the Kings' book of engagements was filled with many other functions, social and diplomatic. On the morning of Tuesday the 25th of April they made a courtesy visit to the Duke of Ormonde, and afterwards appeared before the Commissioners for Trade and Plantations, five members present, who promised all possible assistance and received thanks. The next day His Grace of Ormonde regaled them with a review in Hyde Park of the four troops of Life Guards; a speech of high compliment to the Duke by the sachems on this occasion was printed in the April issue of the leading historical monthly and declared spurious by the leading historical annual. The next evening they were to sup at the Sun Tavern in Threadneedle Street. On Friday the 28th the sachems were 'treated very splendidly' by the New England and New York merchants. The same day, according to the *News Letter* circulated by Ichabod Dawks, the Kings went to see the Hospital of Bethlem in Moor Fields, and also the Work-House in Bishops-gate Street, many of our People Thronging to see them; and amongst the rest a Poor Woman with Child, pretended to Long to Kiss one of their Hands, with which his Indian Majesty being made acquainted, permitted the same, and afterwards gave her a Half Guinea to Buy her some Blankets.

Meanwhile the Queen, on the day after she received these red Americans, had directed the Earl of Sunderland, as Secretary of State for the Southern Department, to refer the sachems' request for missionaries to Thomas Tenison, Archbishop of Canterbury and President of the Society for the Propagation of the Gospel in Foreign Parts. His Grace in turn desired the Society to 'consider what may be the most proper ways of Cultivating that good disposition these Indians seem to be in, for receiving the Christian ffaith, and for sending thither fit Persons for that Purpose, and to report their Opinion without loss of time, that the same may be laid before Her Majesty'. The Board of the Society, convening for its April session on Friday the 21st, heard the letter from Archbishop Tenison (then confined to Lambeth Palace with the gout) enclosing Sunderland's letter and the address of the Kings. It was ordered that a select committee, including Colonel Nicholson, a devoted member, should meet at the archiepiscopal palace on the following Monday at ten of the clock to consider of these high matters.

The Board convened again on the afternoon of the 28th, the Bishop of Norwich in the chair, to hear the report of its committee, whose recommendations became the basis of the Board's resolution to send missionaries to the Indians. A specific programme for converting the Iroquois, worked out by the committee after consulting Schuyler and the sachems, included sending two missionaries and an interpreter and constructing a chapel, a house for the missionaries, and an Indian fort for their

defence. The missionaries would be allowed £150 each
and the interpreter £60, and they would reside at the
principal village of the Mohawks. Furthermore, the missionaries were to promote the study of English by Indian
children and the education of English colonial youth in
the Indian language; sacred texts were to be translated
into the Indian tongue, printed, and dispersed, and the
colonial governors would be urged to execute the laws
against selling intoxicating liquors to the Indians, 'this
being the earnest request of the Sachems themselves'.
And the substance of these resolutions would be framed
into a representation to the Queen, with the added
suggestion that the designs of the Society could not
be carried on for want of a bishop in the plantations, the French having received several great ad-
vantages from their establishment of such an officer at
Quebec.

This large business concluded, the Board was ready to
confer with the Kings, waiting without. The journal of
the Society resumes:

Colonel Nicholson acquainting the Bord that the Indian
Sachems were to Wait on the Society; they were admitted; and
the Lord Bishop of Norwich inform'd them by their Interpreter, that this was the Society to which the Queen had refer'd
the care of sending over Ministers to Instruct their People in
yᵉ Christian Religion; and the Resolutions taken by the Society
in relation to them, were read and explained to them by the
Interpreter, at which the sᵈ. Sachems profest great Satisfaction
and promis't to take care of the Ministers sent to them and
that they wou'd not admit any Jesuites or other ffrench Priests
among them.

The Board, as its final action for the day, ordered that the
sachems be presented '4. Copies of the Bible in 4ᵗᵒ with
the Common Prayer bound handsomly in red Turkey
Leather', the secretary to 'provide them and wait on them
therewith'. Thus did the Indians' request for ministers

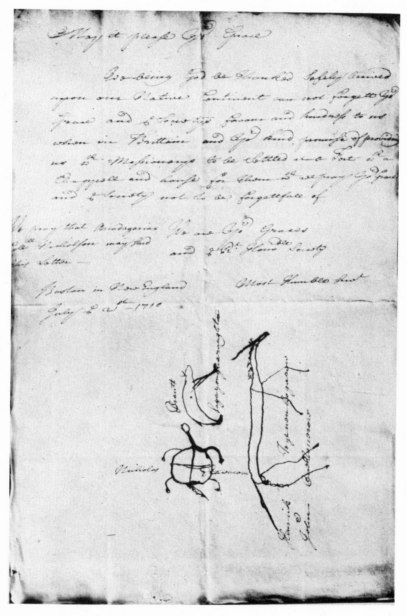

*Letter from the Four Sachems to the Archbishop of Canterbury
signed with their Totem Marks*

receive without delay careful ecclesiastical attention, and they themselves on three occasions dealt directly with representatives of the Society—its secretary, its special committee, and its governing board. Further, a newspaper in Dublin printed a report 'that they will be Baptiz'd before their return, and that her Majesty will stand Godmother to each of them', but nothing more is heard of that kind of ceremony.

On 2 May the sachems addressed to the Society a letter, signed with their totem marks of bear, wolf, and tortoise, expressing satisfaction with the 'usages and answers they received from the Chief Ministers of Christ's Religion in our great Queen's dominions'. On the same day, the Queen having received and approved the ardent representation of the Society, Lord Sunderland forwarded a copy to the Lord Treasurer and expressed Her Majesty's pleasure that all possible assistance be given the Society in its plan to send missionaries and that orders be given for supplying the sum of money necessary to build the fort, chapel, and house. The Crown thereby equalled the fair generosity of the Society in making prompt pledges, to be redeemed at equal leisure.

On 29 April, the day after they were received by the Society, the sachems were dined by William Penn at the Devil Tavern, Charing Cross. And on Sunday the 30th they heard a sermon at St. James's Chapel by the Lord Bishop of London, who then made amends with a magnificent dinner; thence they went to see the great fine house of the Duke of Montague. On the following Tuesday Bernard Lens the younger painted miniatures on ivory of the Kings 'Drawn *by* the life'.

Various activities for which records offer no definite dates had a place somewhere in the Kings' calendar. Between their arrival in London and their day in court, presumably, they marvelled at the plenty of flesh, fish, and fowl in Leadenhall market, and the royal arsenal at the Tower, and they saw a fight of bears at Hockley-in-the-Hole, and later Gresham College, the Exchange and Guildhall, and the dome of St. Paul's, 'survey'd both above and below'. The Blue Coat Boys of Christ's Hospital invited them to supper 'In Respect of their Fame' perhaps the day after the royal reception. They seem to have had more than one conference with the Council of Trade and were entertained by the Archbishop and unspecified persons of quality. At some time they sat to Verelst for portraits commissioned by the Queen, and at another posed for bust portraits by John Faber. And it is possible that they entered the convenient shop of the tradesman in Covent Garden who changed 'his Sign to the four *Indian Kings*, when before he had dwelt at the *Jackanapes on Horseback*'.

Two reputed Kingly occurrences, both benevolent, may be discounted to the vanishing-point. One, which is quite improbable, concerns the high treason of a certain Daniel Demaree, Queen's waterman, who was convicted of animating and assisting the mob in the pulling down of Dr. Burgess's meeting-house as a demonstration of approval for 'High Church and Sacheverell'. His trial had occupied the day the Queen received the sachems, and Demaree, having little to plead save that he had been much in drink, was named guilty, and on 21 April sentenced to death. However, by the Queen's great clemency he was first reprieved then pardoned. On 4 May the antiquary Thomas Hearne in Oxford credited Her Majesty's mercy to the 'Intercession of 4 Indian Kings that are now in England being come from the West-Indies to concert and establish an Allyance against yᵉ French'. But Hearne has no witness for this report, and small is the likelihood that the American and English escorts of the Kings would have permitted their meddling in such a tender matter, that the Indians would or could have volunteered such a plea, and that, in view of Anne's sympathy with the cause of the dashing 'Don Sachevellerio, Knight of the Firebrand', any intercession was necessary anyway.

The other deed of benevolence ascribed to the Kings is legendary—their kindness to the poor Palatines. By 1709 the Rhine country, situate in both the corridor of war and the path of religious persecution; had grown intolerable for the most resolute of its people. Encouraged by a prospect of toleration and security, some thousands of destitute Germans swarmed into England, offering the government large problems in relief, re-employment, and resettlement as they lay encamped at Camberwell and on Blackheath, where for months they served as a Sabbath sight for hordes of true-born Englishmen. The times were hard enough for the English poor without competition from added labourers; the Tories complained out of principle; the Whigs heeded the call of Dissent. A few of these sturdy immigrants were absorbed into the English economy, some died, and the great majority were removed to Ireland, Carolina, and New York. Their connexion with the sachems on tour is the story that one day, while the Kings strolled through the environs of London, they saw these wretched folk on Blackheath and became so touched that with a generous gesture they offered the tract of Schoharie in their own large country as a new homeland for the refugees. This story of the sensible sensibility of such noble savages has been believed and repeated by many of the Palatines to advance their later claims in the Mohawk valley. Without debating whether these chiefs would have donated lands so casually or whether an adviser like Peter Schuyler, himself holder of ample grants of land, would have sanctioned such a major and careless transaction, we know now that the Kings did not even see the 'High Dutch' on Blackheath. The Palatines had boarded transports for New York three months before the arrival of the sachems, and though long delayed in proceeding on their voyage, thus quite missed the visit of the sachems to London.

So much for the Kings in their tour of the Town. At last, about a fortnight after their presentation at court the chiefs possibly had an audience of leave and at such a time offered a polite address of gratitude to the Queen. On the morning of 3 May at three of the clock the Kings departed London and proceeded to Windsor by way of Hampton Court to view the palaces, and on the following morning took coach through the country-side to Southampton, Portsmouth, and embarkation. When the Kings reached port, they could count the gifts—aside from food, lodgings, entertainment, transportation, ceremony, and verbiage—which they had received from a nation willing to pluck the fruits of generosity. Among the Treasury accounts lies the invoice of 'sundry Merchandize bought by order & for account of the Indian Chiefs whereof som sent by Land Carriage address'd to M^r. John Mellish Merch^t in Portsmouth, and the Rest sent to their own Lodging at the Crown & Cusheon in Kingstreet Covent Garden April 1710.' In this list are some fifty entries, a number of the items being by the dozen or the gross. There are many varieties of material—cotton, woollen, and linen, kerseys, duffells, garlix, rowlings, silver orice edging. There is a charge for making 'said Linnen into 43 Shirts at 18d.' There are brass kettles, lead bars, firkins, three dozen looking-glasses, knives (six kinds: large spring, slope pointed, smaller ditto, Scots, horn case, and maple pocket), two dozen large scissors, two dozen smaller ditto, tobacco boxes, two gross coloured twist necklaces, one gross large sorted necklaces, one dozen three-drop pendants sorted, razors, hair horn combs, ivory combs, one gross large jew's-harps, one hat and gun and sword and pair of pistols and trunk apiece, four hundred pounds of gunpowder, ten pounds of vermilion, the Queen's picture, 'a parcel of odd things', and a

'Magick Lanthorn with Pictures'. This plunder, together with charges for packing, porterage, and carriage, cash in specie to the amount of £25, and a commission of £5 to the agent, James Douglas, came to the grand total of £200. Lo these poor Indians as they boarded ship, equipped with several hundredweight of sundry merchandise, each with his copy of the Bible in quarto and the Prayer Book bound handsomely in red Turkey leather. But they left behind several objects, to be gathered into the miscellanies of Sir Hans Sloane's all-gathering collection—a thin, sword-like purification stick for inciting the eruption of foodstuffs, and tump-lines, with headband plain and headband decorated by dyed porcupine quill work, thought by their hosts to be cords for tying prisoners.

The Kings remained in the news after they left London and until they left England, with the shipping dispatches of the principal newspapers carrying details of their homeward exodus. After they arrived at Southampton, Matthew Aylmer, Admiral of the Red and Commander of the Fleet, sent his yacht on the 6th of May to convey them to Spithead, the roadstead where lay his flagship, the *Royal Sovereign*, a first-rate of a hundred guns. The next day they dined with the Admiral so agreeably that they 'tarry'd on board 'till the Evening, and at their Departure received the usual Honours of the Ship'. On Monday the 8th, the wind blowing free north-north-east, they sailed on the *Dragon*, a fourth-rate, which along with other men-of-war was husbanding a fleet of merchant sail. They reached Plymouth two days later, and that evening was marked by the appearance in the air of a 'remarkable, and fiery Apparition' as well as the 'Figure of a Man in the Clouds with a drawn Sword' seen by late strollers in London. The ships left England for America on the morning of the 14th, only to meet contrary winds which forced them to return the same night. Five days later they sailed again from Plymouth.

During these departing days Nicholson did not spare his pen. From Plymouth on the 12th he wrote to Mr. Pringle, the secretary of Lord Sunderland, to acknowledge a letter of the 4th, and to report that he had read Milord's letter to the Indians on board the *Royal Sovereign* in the presence of the Admiral, and to renew the request for military aid, missionaries, and a house, chapel, and fort. During the delay at Plymouth he wrote twice more. When the temporary convoy turned back a hundred leagues off Land's End with any final words to England, Nicholson on 22 May was able again to remind Pringle of hopes for achieving the matters aforetime decided. He likewise could not resign this pacquet without a letter to petition Archbishop Tenison humbly and insistently for action concerning the promised missionaries as well as the chapel, fort, house, and interpreter for them:

for wᵗʰ Humble Submission I think it is of yᵉ last Consequence to have these things gon about as Soon as possible and that the two Missionarys be Sent for these things being promised the Indians they fully rely thereupon and nothing will convince them but Ocular Demonstration and they are for quick Dispatch in all Affairs so that if there be not a Speedy begiñing made I fear they will at least Suspect that what was promised them will not be ꝑformed And that will not only be a point of ill consequence of Religion but of State also.

Nicholson furthermore recommended to His Grace the speedy dispatch of a bishop, without whom the 'Church of England will rather Diminish then Increase in North America'. Also on 22 May from the *Dragon* the sachems sent the Archbishop a letter thanking him and reminding him of the missionaries and the chapel, and Peter Schuyler repeated the Indians' request that 'strong Liquors be debar'd from all Indians in America'. And to the Earl of Sunderland went a letter from the cousins Schuyler to bespeak, because of their perfection in the Indian tongue, the command of the future fort, and another from the sachems themselves expressing thanks for obligations received and satisfaction in Captain Abraham Schuyler as a proper officer of the garrison-to-be.

These messages dispatched, the *Dragon*, the *Falmouth*, and other vessels of war and trade, a regiment of marines, Captain Schuyler, Major Pigeon, Colonel Schuyler, General Nicholson, and the four Kings sailed on and put in at Boston in the New World 15 July 1710.

The Kings had left London and England after such a quadruple regal progress as would take the eyes of folk sharp for a periodic piquancy. The previous year thousands of Rhinelanders had descended, exhibiting the mass misery of displaced persons. Even more exciting, and calling on more powerful feelings, had been the loud and tawdry trial of Dr. Henry Sacheverell, its verdict a bare month gone and its cinders still living. But here was something different—instead of bonfires and tearing down of chapels, shouts for Passive Obedience, sermons pro and tracts con the fiery Doctor, and a cloud of suspicion and bitterness, here were four chieftains from over the very wide sea, allies who looked strong and composed, men novel and rather magnificent, 'Kings' to be seen and talked of. The problems here of Church and State were obvious enough for easy reading; their controversial subtleties would not reach to the man in the mob. The Sacheverell affair had been destructive and exhausting. These Indians from another world were stimulating and restorative.

The Kings had gone home

> having seen our state,
> Our palaces, our ladies, and our pomp
> Of equipage, our gardens, and our sports,
> And heard our music.

Amidst the normal traffic of Anne's England, quickened by the grotesquerie of spectacle and salesmanship, these four men from the Mohawk apparently demeaned themselves with quiet dignity and without a foolish gesture. No word was offered in derogation of their manner, no term of contempt for their manners. In the current opinion they were 'Men of good Presence, and those who have convers'd with them, say, That they have an exquisite Sense, and a quick Apprehension'. As special envoys in this the first official embassy of American sachems they had fulfilled their mission—to gain and give good will and to consolidate the faith that moves ships and persuades war from peace.

THE EMPEROR OF THE SIX NATIONS

Painted by John Verelst
Engraved by John Simon

State and Church

T HE visit of the four sachems, as matter of America, derived from a very present state of colonial affairs, itself a point of circumstance in the prolonged Anglo-Franco-Indian relations. By the time the struggle of the English and the French over the Spanish Succession reached America as Queen Anne's War, northern colonists with the longest view into past and future were realizing that their Indian question must be resolved, and to this question, which included the complex of fur, flag, and faith, with mercantile, Jesuitical Frenchmen of Canada as opponents and the Iroquois Nations as buffer people, the leaders of New York and New England knew but one answer—*Delenda est Canada*.

Before Europeans made any settlements in the country touching that of the Iroquois, Indian Nations had already formed a League covering the lands and waters from the Hudson River through the Mohawk Valley to the Great Lakes. The Confederacy, east to west, of Mohawks, Oneidas, Onondagas, Cayugas, and Senecas was designed for peace by Dekanawidah and Hiawatha, but was soon found good for war. These five united Nations conquered Algonkins, Hurons, Eries, and other uncooperative groups, depending for their success not so much on large bands of fighting men as on the strength of efficient organization, deep determination, and military mobility on widespread waterways. The Iroquois grew, and grew strong, and eventually included the Tuscaroras as the sixth Nation.

The coming of the Dutch produced war with neither the Five Nations of the Mohawk Valley nor the New French of Canada. Peter Stuyvesant had his Indian troubles, to be sure, but with the Iroquois the Hollanders could remain at peace and trade. Any disputes with the Canadians over the undetermined frontier, the competition in the fur trade, and the activities of French missionaries never became so hardy as to make a war; these points of conflict, together with the common problem of the intervening Indians, were left to the English on their occupation in 1664. On the conversion of Nieuw Nederlandt into New York the clash of interest between France and England opened its play on a wild new scene. For two decades the imperial rivalry increased, and by the reign of the second James the ambitions of New York's northern neighbours were clear enough for strong warnings by Governor Dongan to the home government.

Meanwhile the relation of these French to the Indians had presented a compound of exploration, sally, parley, truce, mission, and massacre. The Iroquois, claimed as subjects of the kings of both England and France but controlled by neither, were ready to do business in either direction. At Albany they could exchange their peltry for goods and arms at a better rate than Montreal could offer, but while the French and their native friends controlled the trade routes to the great hunting-lands of the West, the Iroquois suffered a shortage of the furs they could bring to the English frontier post. Moreover, their ancient enmity with the Indian dependents of the French and many of their own sad experiences with French authority reinforced the strong economic reasons of the Five Nations for preferring the English as allies.

King William's War brought major operations as well as small forays by the English and Iroquois. In 1690 the attempt of a coalition of New Yorkers, New Englanders, and Indians simultaneously to attack Quebec by sea and Montreal by lake and land had a calamitous conclusion, and in 1693 an intended expedition by a task force under Sir Francis Wheeler came to nothing. Then the Peace of

Ryswick interrupted the fighting and delayed the solution
to the French-Indian problem, which remained a doubt
into the new century. A war would be expensive to the
colonies in treasure and loss of trade, and the home
government could spare no forces from its current cam-
paigns on the Continent; yet New England was suffering
frequent raids by French and Indian parties, and French
privateering was increasing. Worse, the Iroquois, uncertain ally, unchurched savages, and beaver-bearing hunts-
men, were losing faith in the policy and strength of the
English and gaining belief in their own as the balance of
power.

Hence in 1708, when England had achieved important
victories over Louis le Grand and could follow westward
the course of empire, the American colonists of the north
pressed for renewed action which would protect their
lives and livelihood, retain their strategic Indian alliance,
and advance their cause of Church and State. The resulting project of 1709, centenary year of Henry Hudson's
river voyage, was based on the unfulfilled plan of 1690
for a dual descent upon the French, but it proposed to
add a large and requisite force from England to the marine
assault on Quebec and to add the men of New Jersey and
Pennsylvania to the Indians and soldiers of New York
and Connecticut for the overland thrust at Montreal. This
was the Glorious Enterprise and the only true answer of
the English frontiersmen to the double question: how
to include the Confederacy of the Iroquois and exclude
the Kingdom of France.

Of the three colonial leaders most active in the undertaking of 1709 against the French—Colonel Peter
Schuyler, Colonel Francis Nicholson, and Colonel Samuel
Vetch—Schuyler in name and fame was the man closest
to the visit of the four Indian Kings to London the next
year. Born in 1657, he had become a prominent land-
holder, had won selection as the first Mayor of Albany,

had long been on the board of Indian commissioners, had fought the French and their Indians, had given real aid to several Governors, and had been a Councillor many years. Indeed, he had in his position as President of the Council been acting Governor in 1709 between the regimes of Lord Lovelace and Ingoldsby, and the following year, prior to the arrival of Governor Hunter, would again have assumed the leadership of New York save for his absence with the Kings. But Schuyler's best service to the province and the Crown lay in his informal relations to the Indians—he knew more about Iroquois affairs and was more admired, respected, and trusted by the Iroquois than any other white man of his time, a time when such knowledge of the Indians and co-operation from them carried the highest value to white men. It may have been Peter Schuyler (to the Mohawks 'Quidor' or 'Queder', their version of his very Christian name) who brought forward the idea of sending Indians to England; whoever suggested their visit, Schuyler it was who escorted them across the ocean sea and back to their demesne. While in London this true provincial, it is said, so captured the special attention of the Queen that she presented him with his portrait by Sir Godfrey Kneller, a vase, a gold snuff-box, and a set of silver plate, together with diamonds for his wife, and wished to persuade him to accept of a knighthood. At his return to America Schuyler continued his work as Indian friend and expert until his death in the sixty-seventh year of useful life.

Colonel Francis Nicholson, by two years senior to Schuyler, became his complement in the enterprise of 1709. A cosmopolitan professional administrator of colonial affairs, Nicholson as Lieutenant-Governor of the Dominion of New England under Andros, Lieutenant-Governor of Virginia, Governor of Maryland, and Governor of Virginia had acquired a sizable ability and experience. In 1709 he commanded the land forces in

upper New York; in 1710 as a Brigadier he was Commander-in-Chief of the expedition against Acadia; in
1711, after another promotion, he again led the troops
designed to conquer Montreal. Subsequent to the visit
of the Indians (about whom his knowledge could not
approach that of Schuyler) he was appointed civil Governor of Nova Scotia and finally Governor of South
Carolina. Nicholson pursued broad interests as Fellow of
the Royal Society, very active member of the Society for
the Propagation of the Gospel, and devotee of higher
education in America. The thoroughness and diplomacy
of this 'Governor of Governors' fully assisted the dispatch of the 1709 business and prompted the resumption
of imperial action the following year.

Colonel Samuel Vetch, the careful begetter and general
manager of the Glorious Enterprise of 1709, had lived a
different kind of life. Son of an active Covenanter, Vetch
was bred to initiative and excitement. At the age of
twenty he joined the Paterson scheme to create a great
port at the isthmus of Darien, connecting the East and
the West. After one year in this ambitious failure he sailed
for New York and settled in Albany, soon married the
daughter of Robert Livingston and niece of Schuyler,
and prospered. In 1705 he went to Quebec on an official
mission and studied Canada and the Canada River; the
next year he was in Acadia for other negotiations. His
trading with the French in contraband impeded his career
for the while, but in 1708 Vetch taught the Queen and her
ministry that Canada could be reduced, with all resulting
benefits, by a coincident attack on its two strongholds.
He returned to America the next year bearing royal letters
of instruction to the Governors to aid the expedition as
best they might. Vetch, from his headquarters in Boston,
proceeded to direct the training of the troops and amass
the supplies which were to accompany the British fleet to
Quebec, and acted as co-ordinator of the whole project,

which through no fault of his own was finally put aside. The following year he assisted, again as Adjutant-General, in the Acadian campaign, and became the first military Governor of Nova Scotia. After two years of financial troubles he was removed, but in 1715 became civil Governor for two more years. Vetch died while a prisoner for debt in the King's Bench, 1732. His position in the Glorious Enterprise was central, and he played through his part with tact and courtesy, diligence and skill.

Colonels Schuyler, Nicholson, and Vetch—the sturdy Dutch-American who rightly possessed great authority among the Five Nations, the cultivated and versatile Englishman who six times in five colonies served as sub-head or head of state, and the vigorously venturesome Scotsman who proposed the proper reduction of Canada and guided its progress to the edge of his powers—these colonial collaborators worked together, so far as cool records say, without dispute during the months of this narrative.

To begin the action, Samuel Vetch the summer of 1708 in London directed his experience and persistence and persuasion toward a great campaign against Canada. His programme was a detailed reanimation of the old scheme to proceed synchronously from east and west, a plan well remembered and indeed revived earlier in official representations by high-placed sponsors. On 15 June Vetch requested Lord Sunderland as Secretary of State for the Southern Department to appoint an hour to hear the case against Canada from one who had been there five several times and learned that country better than any other subject of the Crown, and who had been pressed frequently to lay the matter before Parliament but considered such a procedure too public. In a lengthy memorial entitled 'Canada Survey'd' Vetch submitted to Sunderland a careful consideration of the French dominions in

America in their situation, strength, trade, and number, 'more particularly how vastly prejudiciall they are to the British interest, and a method proposed of easily removing them'. He described Canada and her military power, argued nervously for self-interest and self-preservation, emphasized the current loss to the Northern colonies in life and commerce, praised the riches of fur and fish and naval stores to be had. Half of one year's expense in loss of trade, maintenance of troops, and bribing of natives would, if rightly applied, dispossess the French. To accomplish the conquest only two battalions from Britain would be needed, costing no more than their subsistence in Scotland, and only such men-of-war for their protection as were ordinarily employed in attending the colonies or escorting home the fleets. Such a force, joined with a thousand of the best men of New England, should be furnished and transported by sea for Quebec about the end of May or beginning of June while a body of 1,500 men from New York, Connecticut, and Jersey would march with Indians northward directly to Montreal. The victory would make Her Majesty

sole Soveraign of the North Continent of America, and of hundreds of nations of new subjects, who will become intirely obedient to her laws, when they have no preists to poyson them, nor no rivall Monarch to debauch them from her interest and make Canada a noble Colony, exactly calculate for the constitutions and genius of the most Northern of the North Brittains.

A very thorough Scot was Samuel Vetch.

The Council of Trade also received a copy of this comprehensive memorial, dated 27 July, and in order to make a report to the Queen, gave it prompt attention, kept Vetch available for consultation with ten shillings per diem to compensate, also heard Colonel Nicholson, considered the matter at much length, and finally approved the commercial clauses of the scheme, leaving the manner

of acquisition to the military. Vetch submitted an explana-
tory supplement to his proposal, furnishing advice on the
quota for each colony, the sending of arms and ammuni-
tion from the Tower, the provision of transports, pilots,
and supplies, the unification of command, the rendezvous
of English and colonials at Piscataqua, and—after the
victory—the leaving of garrisons and removal of inhabitants. He later presented on request still another memorial,
relating to the number of these inhabitants of Canada,
both French and Indian.

Vetch was successful. The government accepted his
plan, including many of its details, and on the first day
of March 1709 the Queen issued instructions to him. He
was to repair immediately to ship and on arrival in New
York begin the delivery of letters from the Crown to the
several Governors. The quota for New York would be
800 men, including the four standing companies, for New
Jersey 200, Connecticut 350, and Pennsylvania 150. These
1,500 effectives were to be ready at Albany by the middle
of May, with provisions for three months stored at Wood
Creek (a tributary of the great Lake Champaign) and with
a storehouse, boats, and canoes constructed. The Five
Nations and River Indians would be enlisted. The Governors of New England and Rhode Island likewise would
have their 1,200 men, transports, pilots, and provisions
prepared for the arriving of the fleet at Boston. The
governments contributing toward the reduction of
Canada would have a preference with regard to the land
and trade of the country when reduced. Colonel Nicholson, a volunteer, would be admitted to the private consultations with the Governors on methods of execution,
and any necessary preparations not contained in the
instructions would be made with the concurrence of
Nicholson and the pertinent Governor. Such was the
directive of a strategy definite but flexible. In good heart
from such a happy prospect Nicholson and Vetch before

sailing even suggested to Sunderland that after the defeat of the French in Canada the expedition be reinforced by several southern colonies and go against the Spanish at St. Augustine in far-off Florida.

In her letter to Governor Lord Lovelace of New York and New Jersey the Queen charged him to assist 'Our Trusty and Welbeloved' Colonel Vetch after the manner he would propose and to look upon the royal instructions as if direct and positive commands to his Lordship. Somewhat later Lord Sunderland himself informed Lovelace that Her Majesty was fitting out the expedition with a squadron of ships and five regiments to be in Boston by the middle of May, and that Schuyler should be used in negotiations with the Indians, and that Indian spies should be sent to Montreal and Quebec. Concurrently he directed the Governor of Rhode Island to repair to Boston and the Governors of Connecticut and Pennsylvania to the city of New York, there to concert the proper methods for performing the Queen's service. He also informed Robert Dudley, Governor of the Massachusetts Bay and New Hampshire, of Vetch's sailing on the *Dragon* along with some officers and stores for the assistance of the troops to be raised.

Because of a difficult voyage Colonels Vetch and Nicholson left ship on 28 April at Boston instead of at New York as planned, and Cotton Mather promptly considered the great expedition then forming 'another Matter which I had to spread before the Lord'. After precisely two months of less spiritual preparation the two Colonels in a letter to Sunderland spread an abstract of the journal of their proceedings—they had met with Governor Dudley and sent expresses to the other executives, and had taken such measures as preserving security of intelligence, organizing troops, contracting for boats, and establishing communications. Then on to Rhode Island, which had co-operated well. Then to New York,

where they had conferred with Governor Gurdon Saltonstall of Connecticut, Lieutenant-Governor Charles Gookin
of Pennsylvania, and Lieutenant-Governor Richard
Ingoldsby of New York and Jersey in the stead of the late
Lord Lovelace. There Nicholson bowed to persuasion
that he take command of the troops for Montreal, with
Schuyler next in authority. Then to New Jersey, where
the religious principles of the Quakers diminished the
expected aid, and likewise in Pennsylvania. As many
compensatory Indians would be raised as possible, and
the overland force would come to 2,000 Christians and
Indians, with a like number of troops to go by sea. 'So
that in all humane probability nothing can occasion the
designes miscarriage, except the too late comeing of the
fleete.' On the same day, 28 June, Vetch wrote alone to
the Secretaries of State to make his own assurance sure:
he had originally asked that on the success of his proposals he be left Commander-in-Chief of Canada until
the government there should be regularly modelled, and
Sunderland had been pleased to give some assent, but if
the General of the expedition had not already had particular instructions to this desired effect, Vetch hoped that
the ministry would by the first express send his Canadian
commission directly to Quebec. The following day he set
out for Boston from New York, and Nicholson shortly
went with Ingoldsby to Albany, whence he soon wrote
Lord Sunderland on the difficulties of transporting his
expedition and reported that the lateness of the ships was
making people uneasy. The fleet majestical was then
almost two months overdue from England.

Men, stores, and transports continued to stand at the
ready according to plan and promise, waiting for the
force from Britain to arrive in Boston. Spring turned into
summer with no word of the expected ships, and the
colonists became impatient indeed to see the weeks of
warsome weather squandered without explanation and

the Indians growing restive under strain of waitfulness. At length the Council of New York took action: on 21 June 1709 'Coll. Vetch Proposes to have four or five of the most Credible of the five Nations of Indians sent to Boston to see the Fleet and Army that are to come there to go on this Expedition by Sea'. Whereupon it was ordered that Colonel Schuyler do cause the Nations to send such men 'whom they best Confide in for the Purpose aforesaid', that he give them an interpreter and passes to the neighbouring governments, that they touch at Westfield for assistance in furthering their journey and on arrival at Boston apply themselves to Colonel Vetch or in his absence to the Governor, and that they return to Albany after viewing the sea and land forces and give the Iroquois an account thereof. This practical programme for reinforcing the interest of the Indian allies and, through a show of strength at Boston, reassuring them in their choice of the winning side—a sensible and obvious precaution—had a resemblance to, and perhaps a bearing on, the sending of sachems to London, though the later visit added to the purpose of impressing the Indians that of their impressing England. This resolution, proposed by Vetch to be executed by Schuyler, was made more than two months prior to any recommendation to take representatives of the Nations to the English court and nearly four months before official action so to do and ten months before the Kings were presented to the Queen.

On 2 August Vetch sent Sunderland a further summary of progress—he had found the Rhode Island quota in Boston on his return; the transports, flat-bottomed boats, and whale-boats were ready; the troops in Boston could do 'manuall exercise and fire in platoons and battalion equall to most regiments in the service'; and he had had two public fast days kept for the safe and sudden arrival of the fleet. By his last advices the troops in upper New York were well advanced and forts and canoes had been finished, together with a wagon road up to Wood Creek from Albany. He would have proposed an attempt on Port Royal—the French base in Acadia, *Anglice* Nova Scotia—using the ships then in Boston had he but known the English fleet would tarry so long. And he repeated his request to have charge of conquered Canada. In a postscript dated the 12th Vetch dealt with the well-grown colonial anxiety: people were disappointed over losing the great sums of money embarked in the affair and the prospect of lasting happiness and tranquillity as well as advantageous trade; in addition, they were disturbed because word of their preparations would have frighted the French. Once again Vetch hoped he would have his own just reward. Three days later Massachusetts observed another General Fast, upon occasion of the scorching drought and the losses and delay of the expedition.

The first week of August the party of Indians sent by order of New York descended on Boston, where still no fleet had come from the Crown nor reason why. The leaders in Boston set about their chore of influential entertainment. A goodwill dinner for the Mohawks, or Maquas, billed at £1. 16s. 10d., was provided by the province under order of Giles Dyer, who sat in company with them and several other gentlemen. Judge Samuel Sewall twice recorded these Mohawks in his diary:

Augt 9th.

Col. Hobbey's Regiment musters, and the Govr orders the Maquas to be there and see them; and acquainted them there was not one of those Men in Arms they had seen at Roxbury. At night Sir Charles had a great Treat for the Govr, 5 Maquas, &c.

Augt 11th.

The Govr has the 5 Maquas to the Castle and Nantasket to shew them the strength of the Fort and of the Five Men of War. They spread all their Finery to set out their Ships.

The next day Vetch wrote to Nicholson back at Wood Creek reporting a state of readiness but a natural impatience for the advent of the fleet before the lateness of season should rule out the expedition. As to the Indian delegates,

your five Indians with the Interpreters, have been here these Eight days past: And have seen All our Regiments In Arms, Exercise & fire, which they performe Equally to most In the service; yesterday we shewed them the Castle, with fireing Bombs & great guns, and the five men of warr and All the transports In All their glory: they were treated aboard Comadore Martin In the Dragon; All the Ships being covered over with fflaggs, jacks & pennets: And after diner we went with 7 or 8 pinaces full of Gentlemen with them, and lay In the Center of the five Men of warr, while All of them fired, first from their topps & decks In platoons, and then with their great guns upon one an other untill we were all lost In Smoak: they were pleased & surprized beyond expectation; and press us to be gone, saying we have already too manie Men to take All Canada; The Goverment here have given them All fine clothes lac'd with true gold & silver lace, made as ours which will be finished to morrow; Brant and an other goes with us by Sea; I have ordered the Interpreter to transmitt some acct: of it home pr: this Post.

Exactly one month later Vetch described the visit of the tribesmen in a letter to Nicholson which he sent by two of the Indians themselves, who 'seem fully convinc't of the strength and Number of this Countrey farr above Canada' and who were given at a conference in Council the 'most probable reasons we could of the fleets being delayd'. After informing the New York commander that these Indians wanted the forts garrisoned all winter in case the fleet did not arrive, Vetch restated his conviction on the necessity of keeping the Iroquois firm. The mission of Indians to Boston apparently had been worth the trouble and the cost, especially since this latter would be passed on by Governor Dudley to the Lords of Trade in his official account of operational expenses.

Each day of the autumn of 1709 meant to Colonel Vetch, as the director of the separate preparations for a combined campaign, another stint of uncertain busyness. With headquarters in Boston he could confer in person with the Governor of the Massachusetts Bay and New Hampshire, but he must write to the heads of the other participating colonies and to the less accessible Nicholson; he must also make reports of progress to the home government through the Earl of Sunderland. The general scheme of the expedition by converging forces against the two centres of French force had appeared to be good; the colonies, particularly those in New England, had co-operated with each other above their differing grades of separatism and had collected a sufficient quantity of men, money, and material; the Indians, perhaps partly because of the visit to Boston, had so far remained loyal; indeed, the whole business had worked rather well—except for the non-arrival of the British expeditionary force. When would the long overdue and most welcome sail bestir Boston harbour? And why no dispatch concerning the delay? Perhaps the fleet or its intelligence would appear any day, perhaps not soon enough. Perhaps the Grand Expedition must fall; perhaps Port Royal could be conquered as a token victory. Would the English lose the name of hardiness and policy, the French make an attack, and the Indians stand neuter or even turn the tide? In his zeal and uncertainty Colonel Vetch must reach for all his resources of alertness and diplomacy and executive skill in dealing with the collected colonies, the Iroquois, and the overlords in London at this large juncture of colonial affairs.

Early in September came a sign of the general decline of the colonists' position—proposals from Rhode Island and also from Governor Dudley to lessen expenses by disbanding some of the forces. Vetch thought it needful to write the Secretary of State on the 12th of that month, with a postscript of the 22nd, a review of the whole state of things after four months of waiting—the situation at Wood Creek with forts, storehouses, and canoes finished, rations low and clothes worn out, cold weather at hand, and the problem of disbanding or maintaining at a heavy charge; the training of the troops of New England to a high gloss of military discipline; the weight of 'their supposing themselves to be Intirely forgot or Neglected by the Court'. His own disappointment Vetch could not disguise midst his words of deferential frankness.

And As I must acquaint your Lᵈshp: that I have had use for both my Retorick & politiks, to keep up the spirits of the people, under the vast dissappoyntment of the non arivall of the ffleet; so I must confess that I have had Enough a doe to support my selfe, upon the Reflection, that after the vast pains I have been att: (and that with all the success I could have wished for) that I should be so Intirely neglected: as not by the least line to recieve your Lᵈshps: Com̄ands what I should doe with the troops I had raised, and the preparations I had made here: In case some Great reasons had prevented Her Majesties sending the promised ffleet hither; and though I make not the least doubt but that it is upon verry solid & sub-stantiall reasons that the ffleet hath been delayd, yet the great dissappoyntment, this whole Continent is like to meet withall after their hopes had been raised to such a pitch; by so faire a prospect of happiness to them & their posterity, will as your Lᵈshp: may Easily beleeve render them verry uneasy: and not a little with me; who once had so faire a prospect of raising to my selfe a lasting monument amongst them, by being an Instrument of their deliverance. . . .

Vetch could see on the board but one fair and safe move. In a play for time and an effort to gather a concert of opinion he addressed a letter to the Governors of the colonies concerned. After stating the vast cost, their ignorance as to the fleet, the danger of abandoning the up-country forts, and the possible loss of the Indians to the French, he set a meeting of these Governors, accompanied by such of their officers and legislative leaders as they would judge, to consult with him and Colonel Nicholson on the 2nd, 3rd, and 4th of October 'att the most Comodious Centricall place of all the sd Goverments', which he suggested to be New London in Connecticut and later changed to Newport, Rhode Island.

In the meantime the officers under Nicholson at Wood Creek had been composing a letter to Vetch. The authors were Peter Schuyler, William Whiting, John Redknap, John Schuyler, and John Livingston; the latter two also served as couriers. They surveyed the worsening conditions in the New York force, recommended the maintenance of the three forts freshly built, estimated the number necessary to garrison these outposts (with an appended memorandum on stores), and offered a major proposal:

ffurther wee propose (provided always the ffleet doe not arive) that some suitable persons be sent home from the severall Goverments. Truly to Represent the case to the Queen, and Address Her In that behalfe, that wee may yet be enabled to put In Execution what she has with so much Grace, Comanded us to undertake. Respecting—the Reducing of Canada (which designe without any fault of ours is like to prove unsuccessfull) as likewise that two or three of the Sachims & Principall Captains belonging to Each of the five Nations be sent over with them, And Laurence the Interpreter, which wee Judge the most proper methods for securing the Indians In our Interest, and preventing the Incurtions of the Enemy on any part of our Countrey.

The memorial was signed also by the captains of the regiments commanded by Colonels Whiting and Peter Schuyler, in a total of twenty-five names, and got to Vetch well in advance of the Congress of Governors, to

THE KING OF THE GENERETHGARICH

Painted by John Verelst
Engraved by John Simon

whom he could read or summarize it. This proposal to send to the Queen representatives from the colonies and the Five Nations is the initial written suggestion for the delegation to England, and was not made by Nicholson or Vetch or the Governor of any colony but by a group of officers in arms who, restless under delay and doubt, tempered their disappointment by submitting useful ideas for a course of action which might produce the ends long sought but presently dim.

If the broad design of escorting Indian ambassadors to a European court once had an individual inventor, by this date his identity is lost, ideas being as hard to isolate as to originate. Such a scheme was probably of Gallic origin— there was French precedent from the days of Frontenac —and was adopted by the English, growing from mind to mind shrewd and plain. In 1696 John Nelson, a citizen of Boston who had been a captive of the French, suggested counteracting the influence of the enemy by an imitation of their way of transporting 'to France a few of their most eminent and enterprising Indians', and the English had often enough tried to induce chiefs to undertake the voyage, but without success. This recommendation of the encamped officers that Iroquois envoys be sent overseas was but a logical extension of the proposal by Vetch in June that New York send Indians to Boston. Perhaps the advice from Wood Creek was contributed by Peter Schuyler or one of his fellow officers or even by one of the Indians who had visited Boston (or one who wished he had) the month before; of these possibilities Schuyler is the most likely. Whoever conceived the general notion or whoever in the autumn of 1709 gave it new life, the inclusion of Indian representatives in a colonial delegation seemed the best of all possible gambles, having much to win, little to lose.

The Congress of Governors proposed by Vetch suffered a postponement. On 3 October he had word from the frigate *Enterprize* through a ship it had captured but lost company with near the banks of Newfoundland. The lieutenant of the prize recalled that the frigate, out of Plymouth on 4 August, carried an official pacquet. Thus Vetch felt forced to delay the meeting of the Governors lest it take measures inconsistent with the imminent express from Court. The news from Wood Creek in the meantime became more disheartening—sickness and desertion and expectation of the enemy on any day. New York, also, wished to withdraw its troops and, what was more, considered its seaport the best place for a meeting of the Governors.

The all-powerful pacquet, uncertain in contents and time of arrival, would almost certainly resolve the principal problems of the expedition. Vetch and Nicholson waited at Newport, where they urged Governor Dudley's immediate attendance and wrote to Wood Creek to maintain the post and to Lieutenant-Governor Ingoldsby of New York requesting replacements at the camp and his presence at the Congress. At length the pacquet appeared, apparently on the 11th of October, and the Congress convened at Rehoboth in Massachusetts, nearer to Boston than Newport and a more central place after the decision of the New Yorkers not to attend. Present were Vetch and Nicholson and Captain John Moody, Governor Dudley with five councillors and representatives from the Massachusetts Bay and two from New Hampshire, Governor Saltonstall of Connecticut with two in attendance, Governor Samuel Cranston of Rhode Island with seven assistants, and three chief officers of the standing forces, including Sir Charles Hobby. Vetch, of course, promptly acquainted them with the message of the much delayed pacquet, a letter from Lord Sunderland written 1 July. The meat of the news was simply that the Queen had sent the fleet elsewhere (to the Peninsula, it was later learned) and thus the expedition to Canada must be laid aside. However, the forces at hand could be, with the sanction of the Crown and at the discretion of the colonial leaders, employed against Nova Scotia.

The gentlemen deliberated, and on the 14th voted an address to the Queen reviewing the execution of her instructions and praying that the intended expedition be revived and prosecuted with effect the next year, as well as that the article of the Peace preliminaries under negotiation with France on the surrender of American possessions to England be enlarged to include Canada and Nova Scotia, particularly Port Royal, that receptacle of privateers. The Governors further resolved in favour of maintaining the forts in upper New York with garrisons from New Jersey, New York, and Connecticut, and of attacking Port Royal with the forces of Massachusetts, New Hampshire, and Rhode Island and available British men-of-war. And finally, the Congress voted that Colonel Nicholson attend Her Majesty with the representation and address agreed upon, and set forth the losses to the colonies by the diversion of the expedition as well as the future 'great inconvenience' to the colonial governments from the insults of the French and dependent Indians if a descent on them should not proceed the next year; that a gentleman from each of the governments accompany and assist Nicholson; 'And that a Sachim of each tribe of ye five Nations at their election be procured to attend him in his voyage'. This last resolution was the official action which sent the Indian chiefs to England four months later.

The nearest question at that moment, however, concerned not the Indians but the winning of Port Royal, the harbour in Nova Scotia four days' sail from Boston which too often had been a cheerful haven for the French in their raids on English commerce. The answer lay with the accessible men-of-war. Vetch, Nicholson, Dudley, and Moody requested Captain Martin merely to take the

Dragon and *Guernsey* by Port Royal on his way to New-foundland, and asked four other commanders only to delay their expedition to the Bahamas in favour of another the Queen had approved. The replies were nega-tive: the captains had no such authority from the Admiralty. So was Port Royal for a season abandoned to its safety.

With no attack possible for 1709 the leaders set their minds at once on an enterprise to reduce Port Royal the following spring, if the full campaign against Canada could not be remounted. Nicholson was persuaded to take passage at the shortest notice; accompanied by Moody and entrusted with the Governors' address to the Queen and another from the principal inhabitants and merchants at Boston and adjacent places, he sailed on the *Dragon* before the end of October, and Sunderland was informed by Vetch of the hope that some persons from the several colonies would soon follow. Milord Secretary was also given the information that four frigates, five hundred marines, a bomb ketch, and two large mortars would be needed in Boston by the end of March for the conquest of Acadia.

Thus it was that the colonial leaders, a very few days after they knew there would be no immediate attack on the French either major or minor, sent their best spokes-man to London to press a renewal of martial moves at the earliest season. Francis Nicholson accepted the mis-sion, sailing promptly with only one assistant; dispatch prevailed over the desirability of fellow travellers who would represent the subscribing governments and Iro-quois Nations. By such action Nicholson had four months' start on the sachems, an ample period in which to make ready for their reception and one he used with advantage to the cause of the colonists. Before the arrival in London of Schuyler and the four chieftains the home government had agreed at least to a partial revival of the project—the capture of the fortress in Nova Scotia—and had made many preparations.

Meanwhile Colonel Samuel Vetch had been heavily occupied. With armies and supplies and ships and forts, with Indians and the several colonies and the Lords of State, Trade, Treasury, and Admiralty all on his mind, Vetch had perforce given more time to his official work than to his personal advancement, though he was never the man to be shy about his recompense. But with the collapse of the expedition he found more time and need to entertain his own prospects. The final week of October he accordingly wrote to Sunderland, to the Lord Treasurer, and to the Lord President asking in general to be considered for some settled employment in one of the colonial governments and in particular to be left in the chief command of any renewed expedition whether full or partial. Then, a fortnight later, when Nicholson was well away and a greater calm could breed greater doubt, Vetch wrote a second series of requests for patronage. Although he did not burn behind him his claim for commands, he recognized that peace might put a period to the project, and in that pass he besought appointment to one of the vacant Governorships—those, for example, in Virginia, New York, and Maryland. On 16 November he forwarded this request to the Duke of Queensberry, and spent the 18th on letters to four noblemen and two gentlemen well placed for intercession. His prayers were answered the next year, or his efforts remembered, with appointment as the first English Governor of Nova Scotia.

No deputation of gentlemen from the several governments followed Nicholson to London; the colonies could conveniently rest their confidence in his speedy diplomacy and later in the good offices of Schuyler. And the resolution of the Congress of Governors that 'a Sachim of each tribe of ye five Nations at their election be procured to attend him in his voyage' was not carried out precisely,

since chiefs were not procured from each of the Five
Nations and they did not attend Nicholson on his voyage.
But a delegation of Iroquois sachems was selected and
did in time proceed to England.

It is safe to suppose that Schuyler chose the sachems
for the trip on several sensible criteria—appearance,
health, proximity, dependability, willingness, and con-
geniality with him and each other, as well as their status
and prestige. And some faint knowledge of the English
language would have been acceptable. At any rate,
Schuyler in all likelihood knew the four men he elected
and could rely on their conduct. Perhaps they had been
with him at Wood Creek for the expedition. At least one
of them, Brant, had gone to Boston in August in the first
hopefully impressionable delegation, and this view of a
mere town may have inclined him (and others) to see the
great city of the English. That three of the four selected
chiefs were Mohawks was probably a matter of convenience: to the colonists the Mohawk Nation had been
the closest and most important, and a combination of
time, distance, weather, and inclination could easily have
excluded the choice of representatives from the Onondagas, Cayugas, Oneidas, and Senecas despite the resolution of the Congress of Governors. Convenience also
contributed to their nominal possession of royal rank in
England—the translation of 'sachem' into 'King' meant
that their English hosts, unacquainted with the niceties of
Indian organization, were content enough with an easy
mutation of title for leaders of foreign people. The prestige and status of these four Indians in their own country
later were put in question, but their precise native position has here less importance than the fact that exalted
designations were readily conferred upon them in London,
with appropriate honours, to their own probable satisfaction and that of their colonial sponsors, who must
have seen it more politic and sensible to permit such

terms of royalty than to attempt exact explanations of red Indian government.

The number of the sachems in the party has, of all the details in the whole matter, collected the greatest variety of record. Authors of history general and special have stated that there were four Kings, that that were five, that there were six, that one died in England, that one died on board ship, and that one was poisoned. Actually, no more than four Indian chiefs were involved at any stage in the visit to London. No available English document or publication contemporary with the event mentions more than four Kings, and the coeval colonial records all give four as the number of the visiting Indians. The fifth King had his birth and long life most probably from carelessness among early writers on eighteenth-century England and America, or from their reluctance to credit earlier chronicles and use underived records, or from the supposition that a delegation of the Five Nations must have had five representative envoys, as indeed had been the official intention. Likewise from confusion or idle error this apocryphal fifth King perhaps had his death, a decease confirmed by the mature observation that the early allusions were to only four sachems and by the quick conclusion that therefore one of them had died somehow somewhere.

The four Kings can be identified as individuals. In many accounts and pictures they bear their aboriginal names (spelled variously) and distinct titles more grandiose than accurate. Te Yee Neen Ho Ga Prow was called Emperor; his English name was Hendrick. He was the ranking sachem of the quartet, at least in ability and influence. Hendrick became a celebrated American whose name not seldom appears in the annals of conferences with New York officials. Perhaps a Mahican by birth, he became a great leader of the Mohawks, loyal to the British until his death at the battle of Lake George in 1755. It is said that on the Queen's death, Hendrick bore to Governor Hunter the suggestion from the Five Nations for a delegation of chiefs to go to England and return their fealty to the new monarch, but that the Governor tactfully pointed to the absence of a ship and promised to represent their wishes to George I. Hendrick, however, was able to visit England again, about 1740, when George II presented him with an elaborate gold-fringed green coat, in which he sat for his portrait. His fame as orator rivalled that as warrior, and the *Gentleman's Magazine* printed his most famous speech.

Oh Nee Yeath Ton No Prow was Christianized John and dubbed in England King of Ganajahhore. He and Hendrick signed documents with the totem mark of the wolf to show their clan. He had little prominence after the visit.

Sa Ga Yean Qua Prah Ton, of the bear clan, was christened Brant, and called King of the Maquas in London. He died soon after returning from England, a fact not generally known to historians. His highest point of fame is his grandson, the great Joseph Brant, or Thayendanegea.

The fourth sachem was Elow Oh Kaom, or Nicholas, of the tortoise clan, King of the River Nation. He achieved no further eminence. He may have been born either a Schacook or a Mahican, for whom 'River Indian' was a loose term, and had possibly been adopted by the Mohawks.

Colonel Schuyler and his cousin Captain Abraham Schuyler as interpreter reached Boston with the four chiefs in December and were quartered with a Samuel Mears from Christmas Eve to 4 January and from 19 January to 3 February. Mears's bill covers items for lodging, 'breack forst diner & super', rum, green wine, beer, madeira, 'peapers of tobacko', clove water and 'oring water', and use and stabling of horses—a total of twenty-nine-odd pounds. The hiatus of a fortnight in

January, when time lay heavy, represents a hunting trip with Josiah Parker of Cambridge, who was some months later forced to petition his Excellency and the General Court for payment of the expense:

That in the Year 1709, when the four Sagamores of the Maquas were waiting here to Proceed their voyage to Great Britain, the Ships not being ready to Saile, His Excellency the Governour was Pleased to Allow them to go into the ffrontiers to passe Some time in Hunting, and Sent his order to your Pet:ʳ to accompany them, & Provide what was necessary for the accomodation of them, & their Interpreter, & pay the charge thereof. . . .

Parker's bill, less than half of Mears's account, itemizes the cost of horses, subsistence, drink, and a few incidentals (such as an almanac and a beaver hook) for Captain Schuyler and four Mohawks and Parker himself as they made Dunstable and Chelmsford their ports of hunting call.

While the sachems were taking the diversions of the hunt at public expense, Vetch and Dudley thought fit to prepare Lord Sunderland for the imminent visit of the Indians, after a regretful glance toward the cancelled expedition,

the success of which besides All others to the Subjects would have made Her Majesty Sole Empress & peaceable possessor of All the North Continent of America, large enough to forme foure Kingdomes bigger than great Brittain, and to Assure Your Lᵈ:ˢʰᵖ that this Affaire is not only of the last consequence to All the Brittish Inhabitants upon this Continent, but even to the Natives, who are in Allyance with the Crown, the five Nations of Indians In the Neighbourhood of New-York Goverment, and who are the Barrier betwixt them & the ffrench, are so highly sensible of the absolute necessity of extirpating the ffrench, that they have sent their Agents along with Coll: Schyler this length which is five hundred Miles from their own Countrey to Embark here for Brittain to Solicit Her

Majesty upon the same acctt: Alleadging that if the ffrench are
not removed they must either abandon their Countrey, or
Joyne In with them, either of which would be of so fatall
consequence to the Brittish Continent here, as to render it
almost uninhabitable: Your L^d:shp may easily beleeve they are
In Earnest upon the matter; since never any of them could be
prevail'd with before to go over to Brittain upon any acctt:
and now here are four of their cheefe Sachims who have been
here this Month past waiting for a safe passage along with Coll:
Schyler, who all along hath had the cheefe Influence upon
them: but no safe conveyance offering for them untill the
Sayling of the Mast Ships, which will not be untill the latter
end of ffebruary, which wee fearing may be too late, thought
fitt to Acquaint Your L^dshp: of their being thus farr on their
way, and what their errand is, that Your L^dshp: and the
Ministry may take such measures as to your consumate wisdom
shall be Judged best. . . .

This message of 9 January was the Secretary's first knowledge that Indian envoys had commenced their mission.

On the first day of the next month Vetch continued his
report. The zeal of the Five Nations he attributed to their
wise, generous treatment by Nicholson and to Schuyler's
labours among them. He requested that his Lordship
order all due care be taken for the maintenance and clothing of the sachems and that proper presents be made them,
'for they are trew Philosophers that Carry all their Riches
allong with them, taking no Care for more then their
present Subsistance'. Moreover Schuyler, being a stranger
to Europe, had asked to have one of Vetch's officers sent
with him, and Major Pigeon had been so appointed.
On 3 February Vetch and Dudley wrote Sunderland
that Captain Teate had promised the envoys the best
accommodations he could provide on the *Reserve*, which
would occasion him some considerable expense, and
prayed that he be rewarded for the same. One week later
Vetch again wrote the Earl of Sunderland, introducing
the chiefs and Schuyler, the bearer of the letter, to whom

he gave a most excellent character for his work in the
interest of the Queen, his power among the Indians, and
his advance of money for supplies at the Albany garrison.
Vetch also said he had ordered his London agent, James
Douglas, to provide funds for the sachems' transportation
and correct clothing to wear before Her Majesty, as well
as lodging and accommodation until they had waited
upon his Lordship. And then, in an executive mode that
left nothing to chance or another's judgement, Vetch on
the same day wrote the same matter to Mr. Pringle, the
Secretary's secretary, though not with the same deference
due to a man of pedigree. Here he made the supplemen-
tary suggestion that 'It will be requisite the Indians see
as much of the Grandure and Magnificence of Brittan as
possible, for the french endeavour to possess them all
with wonderfull notions of the Grandure and power of
their master'.

About the same time a letter went from Vetch to the
Lord Treasurer presenting Schuyler and the envoys, with
the additional financial statement that New York, 'to
whom it properly belonged to furnish them with all
Necesarys for their Voyage being now a perfect Anarchy,'
had been delinquent, but that he had taken care for their
being properly furnished with such necessaries and clothing. Vetch quite possibly was here referring to the action
of the Massachusetts House of Representatives on 3
February, read and concurred in Council:

This House being Acquainted That the Hon:ᵇˡᵉ Col:º Peter
Schuyler, is about to Embark for Great Britain in the Mast
ffleet, with four of our good friends the Maquas, with Designs
of generall Service, for these Her Maj:ᵗⁱᵉˢ Provinces. RESOLVED
That he be Presented out of the Publick Treasury with the
Sum of Thirty Pounds, towards furnishing his Table, & Con-
veniences for the Said Maquas, in their Voyage.

At last the four Indian chieftains with Schuyler and his
assistant and interpreter sailed from Boston on Her

Majesty's Ship the *Reserve*, Captain Matthew Teate Commander, probably on the last day of February. The *Reserve* put in at a southern Irish port 23 March and arrived in Portsmouth on 2 April, where the Kings were landed and lodged and given 'a sight Of each Rampart, and Bulwark, and Fort' and sent on by stage caravan to the City of Empire. They were in London not long before Easter Monday 10 April 1710, the day Lemuel Gulliver reached the Downs from his voyage to Laputa.

After their stately embassy to England and full reception by the English these four sachems came back to Boston in the *Dragon* on a Saturday, 15 July 1710. With them were Nicholson, the Schuylers, Pigeon, and certain English fighting ships and men. Judge Sewell made watchful record that 'Twas Candle-light before Col. Nicholson got to the Council Chamber; where the Govr and Council waited'. Two days later Colonel Schuyler sent to Governor Dudley a memorandum that the Indians were resolved on Thursday next to set out for their own country and that nine horses and furniture with portmantles would be needed, as well as six pairs of holsters and a guard of ten men with horses as far as Westfield or Springfield. On that Thursday the sachems made their totem marks on a note to the Queen returning hearty thanks for her care in transporting them and for her great favours in England and promise of sending over ministers, with the added hope for a chapel and manse. The following day they likewise thankfully appealed to the Archbishop. The Kings then rode west, officially attended, well laden with gifts, mindful of English iron and stone, and hopeful of their own 'depth of woods embraced' by the green valley of the Mohawk, where no longer could they 'dwindle into royalty'.

The sachems had scarce regained their castles when they were officially reminded of their visit to the Queen. Before they had returned to Massachusetts the new Governor of New York had arrived to undertake a difficult admini-stration—he was Robert Hunter, soldier at Blenheim, gentleman of parts, and favourite of the wits. One of his early acts was to call a conference with sachems of the Five Nations at Albany, where on 7 August some of the leaders of the Iroquois and River Indians, 'particularly those lately come from Great Brittain', waited upon His Excellency when he came ashore and congratulated him on his safe arrival. On the 16th the Governor made various proposals to the assembled sachems, and asked whether they approved the application for missionaries made by those 'who have been lately in England' and whether they desired a garrison and chapel. The Governor suggested that their 'brethren who have been in England and have seen the Great Queen and her Court' must have informed the others as to the mailed might of Britain and the vanity of French boasting. He then delivered presents from the Queen, as pledge of her protection and memorial of their fidelity: a medal for each Nation with the royal effigy on one side and the latest victory on the other, and also her picture on silver, twenty to each Nation, to be given to the chief warriors as a token of their readiness to fight under her banner against the common enemy. On the 19th Hunter had his reply: 'Some of our Brethren have been lately in England, and altho' they were natives of ye Mohogs' Nation, yet we are as well satisfy'd as if there had been one from each of ye 5 Nations, being all united; they have seen ye Great Queen and her Court, and been very well treated, for wh. we are very thankfull.' The Indians confirmed their desire for missionaries, fort, and chapel, and gave thanks for the medals and silver. The next day the Indians addressed the Governor again on 'something forgott in ye publick propositions yester-day' concerning the two missionaries promised by Her Majesty 'when we were in England'. One of them, the sachems had then suggested to the Queen, might well be

Mr. Freeman, minister at Schenectady; Her Majesty having approved of this proposal, the sachems desired him to come to them at least until the appearance of a missionary from England. In this speech both the topic under hand and the use of the first personal pronoun say that sachems of the visit themselves presented this addendum.

Nicholson had returned to America on the *Dragon* not so much to escort the sachems (Schuyler still acting as their *doyen* on the westward voyage) as to lead a secondary attack against the French. On the collapse of the great pincer movement in the previous year the Congress of Governors, be it recalled, had deliberated an immediate descent on Port Royal, Acadian base of the French raiders, but for lack of naval co-operation this assault did not get under way. Hence the colonial leaders had been anxious for Nicholson to take ship for London as early as possible 'In order to hasten over Assistance In the spring to Reduce at least Port Royall if not Canada'. Permission to subdue Acadia was all that Nicholson could gain. With royal instructions for the reduction of Port Royal and with his own commission as General and Commander-in-Chief of the forces, Nicholson brought from England, besides the four Indian Kings and the others in the ambassadorial party, 400 marines, nigh half of them new raised. He proceeded to the preparations which the home government had not made in advance. On 18 September 1710, Nicholson and Vetch set sail with the *Dragon*, *Falmouth*, several other ships of the line, a number of subsidiary vessels, the English marines, and four regiments of New Englishmen. The French, ill prepared for even this moderate attack, soon requested a truce, and Port Royal became the Queen's own Annapolis Royal, confirmed to the English by the Treaty of Utrecht. Governor Dudley proclaimed a General Thanksgiving throughout the Massachusetts Bay and New Hampshire for the general health, a very plentiful harvest, and the military success. This Anglicizing of Acadia was the sole English gain in America during the war years 1709-11, and though the Kings returned with the men and ships for this expedition, it had been determined and instructed before their arrival in England.

While the sachems were still in London and while Nicholson was also there, completing plans for the attack on Acadia, an effort was being made by English men of state to expand the imminent expedition into a larger campaign against Canada. The day after the Queen gave audience to her Indian Kings, Godolphin, the Lord Treasurer and leading minister, wrote the Duke of Marlborough in Flanders that the Cabinet Council seemed inclined, with the resumption of Continental hostilities, to renew their larger design on Canada of the previous year. He believed such work would be put in execution as soon as they could be free from all doubts concerning Scotland. A few days later, on a day in the centre of the Kings' round of entertainment, Godolphin wrote with more particularity—six regiments in England could be spared for pressing service, of which the Council seemed determined to send five for the North American conquest and the other to North Britain, where the Pretender was expected the next month. Not for long did this determination stand firm, but a decision to send these troops westward remained a potentiality until July while the government blew warm and cool. As soon as the Duke of Marlborough heard of the plan he made positive his dissent, calling as reasons the great expense, the ruining of regiments transported oversea, and the inability of any such enterprise to advance the peace or gain more for England in many years of travail than would one dash of a pen on a treaty. Soon a rival appeared to the colonial excursion—a manœuvre against the French by a descent on one of their nearest seaports, a project wherein

Marlborough might employ the five regiments. This project Godolphin on 2 May suggested to the Captain-General, his close friend and long ally who had a way of winning battles, and of it he wrote frequently until August, wrote with fervour for its aid to Queen, to country, and to Whigs. The Duke demurred and questioned: he had to consider the movements of his enemy, and his own political place amid the disputes in England counselled caution to attempt nothing but what was sure to succeed. In the end he made no move to use the waiting troops. By June Godolphin could detect less fondness among his colleagues for dispatching the ready regiments so far from home, and by July the season seemed too far gone and the winds had turned contrary, and there were further alarms of a Jacobite movement in Scotland.

Sunderland, meanwhile, had gone ahead with plans: stores and transports were ordered, and Lieutenant-General Viscount Shannon was named Commander with instructions to go to Boston, there call a council of war and agree on the most proper methods of acting in conjunction with the forces of New York and New England against Quebec and other places on the St. Lawrence. But the government were the prisoners of circumstance that summer of 1710, a time not ripe for high exploits. The state of the war, the flux of public opinion, the furore of the Sacheverell affair, the temper of the Queen, the side-stairs diplomacy of Mrs. Masham and Mr. Harley, the personalities of the great Whig lords, the lack of unity or firmness within the ministry—all these and more came to frustrate consistent decision and persistent execution. The sudden removal of Sunderland as Secretary of State on 14 June and the rude dismissal from the Queen's service of Godolphin on 8 August marked a season not happy for the launching of squadrons toward a distant conquest, aside from the matter of marine meteorology and rumours of a rising for 'King' James. On the final

THE KING OF THE MAQUAS

Painted by John Verelst
Engraved by John Simon

day of August the Earl of Dartmouth as Sunderland's
successor addressed letters to Nicholson, Vetch, and the
Governors of New York and New England to say of this
expedition that Her Majesty had been forced to lay it
aside 'for the present by reason of the contrary winds
which happen'd, when the season was proper for the
Fleet to sayle, and in regard of other important services
which intervened'. This the third in a series of undertakings against the colonial French was thus abandoned,
like the first, after much conference and business and no
military action, and even before the achievement of the
second enterprise. In regard of the sachems, their visit
may have begun too late to induce this further effort of
1710 but could give it a strong encouragement.

    After the capture of Nova Scotia Nicholson returned
to England to urge another land-and-sea, English-
colonial war upon Canada, although Whiggish New
England could scarcely hope that the new Tory England
would go against the French in the New World. But
Nicholson found favourable the winds of politics: the
Tory policy towards Canada had become partisan in that
it strove not to forsake but to surpass the Whig effort, and
so by a turn of statecraft English America stood to gain
by the fall of Godolphin's ministry. Despite the rise of
Harley the fame of Marlborough had remained bright in
many quarters, or luminous enough to disturb his opponents. The winning of the West would at once contrast
with the failure of the Whigs in 1709 and their small
success of 1710, and would balance the popular victories
of the great Duke, who preferred European to American
operations. Also, the transfer of some of his veterans to
colonial duty would lessen his power and renown. The
French, at home forspent, could make no major offensive
and could ill defend their far colony. Henry St. John as
the new Secretary of State for the Northern Department
yearned for green laurels; the Queen had lost no interest

in defending her faith abroad; and the Tories set value on such imperial profits as would not be shared with some Continental ally. The long, strong arguments of colonial leaders had finally reached well into the English administrative mind, and the Indian Kings in person had brought the American problem to court and capital. Thus in 1711 the accomplishment of a great colonial triumph appeared the best of not over-bold strokes from the political, military, economic, and religious coigns of vantage, or so it seemed to the party in power, and so it would seem now had it come off. But well begun was never more than half done, and here was something less than half.

St. John on receiving the seals of State directed his sharp mind toward this verdict for open colonial war, and by his own admission formed the whole design of the new undertaking and singly carried its management. Harley at the head of the ministry was hesitant, but unable to diminish the energy of St. John, who assured his superior that he was 'not light or whimsical in this project'. Shortly Harley's penknife wounds from the miserable Guiscard removed his shadow for a season, and St. John was able to proceed unhindered. Ships, stores, troops were gathered and commanders were selected, all in a secrecy meant to perplex the enemy abroad and opponents at home. When Nicholson returned to Boston in June with renewed royal instructions to the northern colonies to prepare their quotas against the coming of the new army and fleet, anti-Canadian hopes burned high. This time the armed force left England and arrived at Boston, indeed only a good fortnight after its herald, in the largest American enterprise so far attempted by England. The army, numbering with two regiments from New England near 7,000 men, was under Brigadier John Hill, the newly promoted brother of Mrs. Abigail Masham, herself newly promoted to the Queen's confidence in the room of the grand Duchess of

Marlborough. The fleet, consisting of fifteen fighting ships
and forty sail of transports and supporting vessels, English
and colonial, had Sir Hoveden Walker for Admiral.
Vetch was called from his Governor's chair in Annapolis
to lead the New Englanders. In Boston the raising of
money, collection of provisions, and dealing with de-
serters produced difficulties, but these were in time dis-
solved.

On 22 July three Mohawk sachems arrived in Boston
as a deputation to see for themselves whether ships and
troops had really come. The next day Nicholson brought
them to Walker, who amazed them with the bigness of
his ship and delighted them with wine, music, and sea-
men dancing; they answered 'in their Way of Dancing,
which was a very different Manner to any thing ever seen
in *Europe*; for each in his turn sung a Song and danced,
while the rest sate down and hum'd and hollow'd at distinct Periods of his Dance, with a Tone very odd and
loud, but yet in Time'. Then came an exchange of speeches
and drinks to the Queen, and when they went away the
Admiral gave them cheers and guns. Governor Dudley
proclaimed a General Fast, by the Queen's instructions,
for 26 July as well as the last Thursday of every month
during the expedition, in order that divine conduct
might be granted the General and the Admiral. The Fast
filled the sails, and on 30 July this minor armada set
forth from Nantasket.

General Nicholson proceeded then to Albany, whence
he would lead against Montreal, by the old plan of a
double attack, an overland army of provincials, trans-
planted Palatines, and Indians. These last must be kept
content or, better, militantly anti-French; but what would
hold them faithful? Since the tribal headmen had long
been accustomed to receiving gifts as perquisites of their
leadership—money, arms, fabrics, trinkets, potables, and
European curiosa—what would be more persuasive than

some memento of the visit which the Indian Kings had only recently made to London? In August Governor Hunter addressed an assembly of sachems, with Schuyler and Nicholson present; the latter 'being arrived safe from England has brought the Pictures of the 4 Indians that were in great Brittain last year, & gave each Nation a sett & 4 in Frames with glasses over them to be hung up in the Onnondage Castle the centre of the 5 nations where they always meet. . . .' Dispersal of such proper presents was enlarged, the record runs, to include sets of the pictures in frames to the Council chambers at New York and Boston, and eight sets without frames to New York and Boston and four each to New Jersey, New Hampshire, Connecticut, Rhode Island, and Pennsylvania to be disposed among the Assembly and Council as the Governors thought fit, with one set, also frameless, to the Governors of Maryland and Virginia to be hung up in the Council and to each of the four former Kings— in all, twelve pictures in frames and 192 without.

Canada lay open to conquest, prepared by word though not in power, and to Governor Saltonstall in Connecticut everything looked 'with a fair prospect of good success to her Majesty's arms'. But the St. Lawrence was a French water with its own unfriendly winds and tides, and soon the end of English promise. Admiral Walker became timorous; his pilotage was untrusted or untrustworthy; ships ran on breakers at Egg Island; seven hundred Englishmen were drowned. A hundred leagues from the Heights of Abraham, Walker abandoned the surmounting of Quebec or even a try for Placentia in Newfoundland. On 16 September he turned for home unprosperous, and on arrival lost his flagship and papers by explosion. General Hill of course had no chance to prove his military science. Charges against the colonists of hindering the operation survived the debacle and made their grief the worse. Canada remained French except for Nova Scotia, which but for the grand fiasco might have suffered a counter-attack.

Upon receipt of the dismal intelligence from the Canada River Nicholson's army in northern New York was for the second time in two years compelled to resign its objective. Promptly he made further gifts, in the house of Schuyler, to sachems of the Iroquois, hoping to soften their disappointment and replace the expected Canadian booty. These presents, the staple of amity, had the variety of usefulness and symbolism: one Queen Anne's guinea in memory of Her Majesty; in memory of Nicholson one cane with an amber head, which when warm would become attractive and betoken the warmth of his love and theirs and the desire to draw each to the other; one multiplying glass to represent the fraud of the French in making a few things seem many; a more practical pair of pocket brass musquetoons and one long gun to show the French how well the Indians are armed; two barrels of beer to retain the Queen's health; and 'One of ye Oxford Almanack's with ye cutt made upon their late sending the four embassadors for England, shewing H.M. tender regard for them.'

The four projects against the French in Canada had had various conclusions. In 1709 a great marshalling of colonial resources in Boston and at Lake Champaign was brought to naught because the promised English fleet had been diverted to another sea; with no soldier on the march against Montreal and no ship under way toward Quebec, the colonists knew only defeat to plan and hope, to time and treasure. In 1710, in the only successful enterprise of four in three successive years, a minor sally captured Acadia, which thenceforward remained English and an aid to English waterways. Also in 1710 an attempt to renew the full assault became diluted by counter proposals and a poor political climate into nothingness. And in 1711 a strong and likely naval enterprise, to be supported by a competent inland attack, was so weakly directed as to make a quick end in self-defeat. Small gain, large loss. The divine ruler, it was said by some, had ordained it so: England was not destined to have the continent. New York and New England still faced the French and their Indians. The Whigs and the Tories both had failed the colonists, who, being neighbours to the peril of Canada, gave better thought and work to the operations than did the Crown and its servants at home. But the colonies had learned some measure of intercolonial action and perceived exercises in imperial irresponsibility. England was little stronger, with a Peace of the Spanish Succession to sign and a War of the English Succession to forestall. Canada waited for Amherst and Wolfe.

The London visit of the Kings had a different relation to each of these four designs on the lands of Louis the Magnificent. First, although the recommendation to send Indians to court was made before news came that the 1709 expedition had been abandoned, this proposal was adopted as a result of that disappointment. Second, the decision in London the following year in favour of an Acadian incursion was handed down prior to the Kings' arrival in England, but their presence in London could reinforce the wisdom and popularity of that mild resolution. Third, the deliberations later the same year to throw a full force against Canada were resumed perhaps before the arrival of the sachems, but the progress of those counsels may have been in some wise affected by the current public excitement over the visiting potentates. Fourth, the major project of 1711 had the benefit of a somewhat more mature Indian influence, albeit far second to that of personal ambition and partisan aspiration by English statesmen. Thus for three of the four undertakings the embassy of the Kings provided the general aid of publishing the Indian question—a main motive of the colonists in promoting the visit. The leaders in America knew that though matters of high statecraft were determined in camera, chancellors can be very susceptible to spectacle, and that the people might assist a ministry by approving an action for which they felt enough warmth. The desired action was not something novel or radical, but a renewal only of an effort heedfully approved and prepared, then deflected. In presenting themselves as dignified deputies of the strong red men, living between English Americans and the fearsome French, choosing the former as trading ally and requiring British aid against a common foe, the sachems created the public, political influence they were brought to make. The complementary motive—that of strengthening the faithfulness of the Iroquois by fear and friendship—also was realized: that is, the Confederacy and especially the Mohawks did not turn to the French, though to be sure other and good reasons for a continued alliance came and went. It is, on the whole, fair to think that the link formed by this long, strange journey of these foreign envoys became one, and not the weakest one, in the chain of loyalty of Indian to England.

In the affairs of Church, never separate from those of State, the national rivalry between France and England employed religion as an agent. Under the encouragement of the Governors of Canada the Jesuits had often taken themselves deep into the forests of the Iroquois, and in their ecclesiastical colonizing had rejoiced to live with the Indians or even to die under their torture. Protestant ministers, who did a work valiant and valuable in the seaboard colonies, were, for whatever reason, content with less travel and fewer pains than their Roman colleagues. Those Frenchmen of God spread the glory of France along with their gospel so that the Indians, body and mind and soul, could be true children of Pope and King, but certain churchly teachings, reaching Anglican ears, appeared at times inaccurate, impertinent, and irreverent. There was such a story as this, of great currency in the era of Anne:

The Popish Missionaries take indefatigable Pains to convert them; but to give you an Instance of the Doctrine they teach them, it will be enough to observe in this Place two of the Questions of their Catechism they teach to those Indians. Question, *Where was the Saviour of the World born?* Answer, *In France.* Question, *Who Crucify'd the Saviour of the World?* Answer, *The English.* This is I think sufficient that in Point of Interest as well as Religion we are obliged to undeceive that People, seeing the French, under Pretence of teaching them the Christian Religion, inspire them with an irreconcilable Hatred for our Nation.

With or without such a catechism the Black Robes were effective, at least enough so to persuade colonial authorities to request their own missionaries for the Indians, where ministers would be of good service as well to improve the interest of England as to promote religion.

In 1701 the Society for the Propagation of the Gospel in Foreign Parts received its royal charter, and two years later, on receipt of an order-in-council which pointedly recognized that instruction in the true faith might confirm the Iroquois in their duty to Her Majesty, the Society agreed to send missionaries to the Five Nations. In 1704 the Reverend Thoroughgood Moore became the first English missionary to the Mohawks. The Indians expressed pleasure at his arrival in Albany, and Mr. Moore was eager. He desired to be accepted among his charges, and he offered to commit to their custody a young kinsman, but Mr. Moore had to learn that sudden decisions were not a Mohawk custom. After a twelvemonth of native delays and excuses he was ready to abandon the work. In his full report of disillusionment he strongly reasoned that the colonists themselves had great need for the care of the Society and that the behaviour of such

Christians as the Indians saw gave them a sad notion of
Christianity. He further observed that because of distempers introduced by Christians and the always cruel
ends of strong liquors, the Indians were wasting away like
snow against the sun 'So that very probably forty years
hence there will be scarce an Indian seen in our America.'
The Society granted Mr. Moore's request for a transfer
to New Jersey, and the Mohawks were left without a
missionary until 1709, when the Reverend Thomas
Barclay was appointed to instruct them in addition to
his duties as chaplain of the Albany and Schenectady
garrisons.

Thus by 1710 the work of the Society for the Propagation of the Gospel had once failed among the Mohawks
and was currently being conducted in a minor manner.
The requests of the sachems in London therefore came
opportunely in time and place, and the envoys won a
quick and generous reception, which looked to have a
large and speedy outcome. After the Kings left London,
they and the commitments made them by the Society
became matter for report at the next five monthly meetings of its Board, May through September—the secretary had delivered the Bibles to the chiefs, who had given
thanks; their letters from the *Dragon* were communicated;
the Lord Treasurer was waited upon and a memorial laid
before him—with but little satisfaction—for the sum of
money proper to fulfill the promises of fort, chapel, and
house for the missionary; and names were proposed of
candidates for missionary.

On 5 January 1711 Nicholson, back in London from
the victory at Nova Scotia, delivered to the Board the
letter of the sachems dated 21 July at Boston, begging
to remind the Society of its pledges, and at the same meeting a clergyman named Bishop was nominated to fulfil
one pledge. A fortnight later the Board again discussed
ways of providing for the sachems, and a letter concerning

his work was read from Mr. Barclay, still giving a part of his time to the Mohawks. He had said that 'the Great Prince Hendrick that was so honour'd in England can't command ten Men, and the other 3. were no Sachems', to which Nicholson answered that there were 'several things untruly asserted in the said Letter especially relating to the Sachems'. On the first day of February the Board desired Nicholson to put the Archbishop 'in mind of recommending two Missionarys to be sent as soon as possible to the Sachems, who have by the said Colonel Nicholson earnestly press't the performance of the Queen's and Society's promise to them'. Only a week later Nicholson reported his interview with His Grace the President of the Society, who was pleased to desire a list of the missionaries already in the plantations from which to choose a man qualified for the service. This the Society agreed to do, and decided also that its financial circumstances would then permit of only one missionary to the Indians. On 21 March the Archbishop wrote to the sachems to acknowledge their letter from Boston, written eight months earlier, to assure them that missionaries would be sent when the fort, chapel, and house were fit to receive them, and to say that a sum of money had been deposited for construction expense and that he could be drawn upon for the larger remainder to make up the total to £400, the amount promised by the Queen.

Before the end of the busy year 1710 Peter Schuyler had laid out the ground for the fort, chapel, and parsonage and made an estimate of expense, and in time his recommendations reached the Society. At last, on 9 October 1711, Nicholson, Governor Hunter, and the Commissioners of Indian Affairs had a meeting whereat Hendrick presented a letter for the Archbishop; and at this conference, dull with new disappointment over the recent miscarrying of military affairs, the building of forts and coming of missionaries were discussed. Two days later the indenture was signed between Hunter and Nicholson as one party and four carpenters of Schenectady as the other for the building of two log forts and chapels in the Mohawk country and the Onondaga for the sum of £1,000. The fort was to be 150 feet square with curtains twelve feet high and scaffolds five feet wide along each curtain and a two-storied blockhouse at each corner twenty-four feet square. In the centre would be the chapel, ten feet high and twenty-four square, with garret and cellar. The Mohawk garrison, enclosing the chapel and manse on the south bank of the Mohawk River as it accepts the Schoharie, was completed in August of 1712 despite an Indian assault on the carpenters, and the Governor stationed at the future Fort Hunter '20 private men and an officer'. In October Mr. Barclay went from Albany to the new church; he chose Matthew xxi. 13 as his text, following the desire of the sachems that he preach against profanation of God's house, 'some being so Impious as to make a Slaughter House of it'. Nothing remains today of the original group of buildings, but the site is marked with a metal plaque and in season by the concourse of a wild flower uncommonly well-named for this history—Queen Anne's Lace. Later and at some distance was built the permanent house for the missionary, farther from the river and on higher ground, two stories of limestone, port-holed, still habitable, and now under good cover of an elm and two birches.

For Queen Anne's Chapel Her Majesty sent, as was her way, a set of rich communion plate—a salver, a bason, a chalice, a paten, and two flagons—inscribed with the royal cipher and coat-of-arms and bearing the almost regal hallmark of the silversmith Francis Garthorne. The Queen sent also sumptuous furniture—an altar cloth, pulpit cloth, communion table cloth, two damask napkins, carpet for the communion table, large cushion with tassels for the pulpit, and small cushion for the desk—

as well as a Holland surplice, one large Bible, two Common Prayer Books, one book of homilies, and a painting of Her Majesty's arms on canvas. Archbishop Tenison presented a dozen large octavo Bibles very finely bound and two tables painted of the Commandments, Lord's Prayer, and Creed, together with ninety-seven prints of the Queen's effigy and arms for distribution among the Indians. The Society gave 'a Table of their Seal finely painted in proper Colours' to be fixed in the chapel, and five dozen quarto and octavo sermons for the province.

The new missionary selected and appointed in 1712, nearly two years after the personal appearance of the Kings before the Board, was the Reverend William Andrews, 'who has a very good Character, is an un-married Person, hath been in the Plantations, and has some understanding of the Indian Language'. Whereupon the Archbishop wrote to the sachems that soon they would see the result of their wise application to the royal bounty in the person of a missionary, to whom they would certainly give protection and encouragement, and on 13 November Mr. Andrews arrived at Albany, where he was made welcome by five of the principal chiefs, including Emperor Hendrick. On the 15th, at a great meeting of important people and many Indians, Mr. Andrews publicly opened his ministry; he made a short address on the de-sign of his mission, and Hendrick spoke in gratitude to God, Nicholson, the Queen, 'their Ghostly Father his Grace the Arch Bishop and the rest of the Spiritual Sachems of that Godly Body'. Hendrick said further that the Mohawks desired that none of their land be clandes-tinely purchased and that they not be brought under the yoke of tithes. Mr. Andrews replied that he 'was not come for the lucure of their land nor to lay burdons on them but to Instruct them in the true Christian Religion', and as for the fear that the minister would claim a tenth of

their lands and goods, the Honourable Society had taken
care to pay him.

A week later the missionary travelled to the new establishment at the Mohawk castle, some forty miles by river
north and west of Albany, escorted by Mr. Barclay and
others. The Indians there visited him in numbers and
showed abundance of joy at his arrival and a disposition
to come to the chapel for prayers and religious instruction
'in a Catechetical Way' each Wednesday and Lordsday.
Early in his ministry, however, Mr. Andrews learned
some of the obstacles which would bedevil his term of
service—the Dutch traders, fearful that the settling of a
minister among the Indians might interrupt improper
trade and lessen their gains, worked to make divisions
among the Indians and incite them against the missionary,
spreading the suspicion that a Queen's fort for giving
protection to her chapel would be as well a Queen's fort
for the taking of territory; the deceitful dealings of these
and other Christians provided poor examples of the best
fruits of the white man's religion; the male Mohawks were
inclined to take too much rum; and Indian primers for
teaching the children would have to be supplied, with
some trinkets to give progressive encouragement. Soon
the question of instructing the Mohawk children in the
Indian language or the English was answered by the
parents in favour of their own, which in a sense was just
as well because an understanding of English would but
give a better opportunity to learn new vices. In addition,
translations of sacred and ecclesiastical texts would be
required, and as the interpreter was a Dutchman competent in the Iroquois dialects but deficient in English,
an interpreter for the interpreter would likewise be necessary.

After a circuit of the seasons, with the extreme coldness
and deep snows of winter, the flies and mosquitoes of
summer, and the rattlesnakes, Mr. Andrews could say

that 'There is no manner of pleasure to be proposed by being here, but only the hopes of doeing some good among these poor dark ignorant Creatures.' However, for a time the efforts of the missionary and his two assistants went well, or well in consideration of the difficulties: the children learned readily, some of the adults continued to receive instruction in the articles of faith and rules of life, and such Indians as possessed knowledge of English gave attendance in the small, well-adorned chapel. But most of the early difficulties continued. Moreover, the necessity of feeding the Indians, 'who are Constant Visitors for their Bellies', particularly the giving of victuals to the children as a stimulus to learning, proved too heavy for the stipend of the missionary, who lamented his lack of means better to feed and clothe the needy. And ever in opposition to the labours of his patient ministry were the activities of the French and the Jesuits. Also there were Indian threats to his life, and the advent of the Tuscaroras from Carolina with tales of English persecution produced rumours of further mischief.

During the second spring of his mission Mr. Andrews, to try what he could do among another Nation, travelled to an Oneida castle above one hundred miles away, which had, as he reported, 'only a small rough Indian Path to it: We lay several Nights in the Woods agoing, and on a bear Skin when we came there, but I don't matter any fatigue or hardship I undergo; if it shall please God to bless my endeavours among those poor bewildred People.' The Oneidas and their sachems received him warmly, and he baptized nineteen, to most of whom he gave good Biblical names, like Adam, Aaron, Luke, before returning to the Mohawks. However, after he left the Oneidas, some of the children he had baptized died and he was accused of poisoning them, so his intended visit the next year was cancelled lest he be murdered.

Mr. Andrews worked, indeed, with diligence, sense, and generosity, and his long letters to his sponsors speak a sound heart and clear eye. But in time the Mohawks wearied of being taught, and forgot in the forest what they had learned in his school. The success of his pastoral care declined, and the chapel lost the Godly influence it was built to have and for a season achieved. Mr. Andrews was finally defeated by forces too many and old and strong and subtle for his brave work—after six years of devotion he officially made surrender by asking a removal, to which the Society agreed with much reluctance and only after an examination of the case by its member, Governor Hunter.

So ended the first major mission of the English Church to the Mohawks, a physical and spiritual result of the overtures by the four Kings, and one of the early monuments in the concerted propagation among the red Indians of the gospel according to the Anglican persuasion. The disappointment of the Society may be read on the spirited page of its secretary and first historian, David Humphreys:

It is indeed Matter of great Wonder, that these wretched People, who have lived joining to the *English* Settlements so many Years, and cannot but observe that the *English*, by Agriculture, raise Provisions out of a small Spot of Ground, to support in Plenty great Numbers of People; whereas they by their Hunting, cannot get a wretched Subsistance out of all their Wildernesses of several Hundred Leagues in Extent; should still refuse to till their Ground, or learn any manual Art; should still live a bestial Life, insensible of Shame or Glory. It is true, the *English* have taken from them exceeding large Countries, yet this, far from being a Prejudice, would be a vast Advantage to them, if they would but learn the *English* Language, Arts, and Industry. They have still an immense Extent of Land, part of which, if duly cultivated, is able to maintain many Millions of People more than they are. It might have been imagined the *Sachems*, those petty Kings, who were in *England* in the late Queen's Time, should have been so strongly affected with seeing the Grandeur, Pleasure, and Plenty of this Nation, that when they came to their own Countries, they would have tried to reduce their People to a polite Life; would have employ'd their whole Power to expel that rude Barbarism, and introduce Arts, Manners, and Religion. But the contrary happened, they sunk themselves into their old brutal Life, and tho' they had seen this great City, when they came to their own Woods, they were all Savages again.

It is true the well-travelled sachems, however affected by their own glorious enterprise, wrought no revolution in their native land. But theirs is no history of degradation or brutality. Brant died two months after reaching home from England. Nicholas and John apparently found their way back to obscurity unobserved. Hendrick for many years continued to take some major part in Indian relations. In the autumn of 1722, for example, not long before the stricture by Humphreys, Hendrick without doubt was one of seven Mohawks who went to Boston to mediate between the French Indians and the colonists. At a 'magnificent feast they made to the 7 Indian Princes of the Erocoi Mohoks' he was seen by one Thomas More, not a man of church or state or a sainted knight of Utopia but a collector of natural specimens, called the Pilgrim Botanist. More wrote to William Sherard, one of his employers in London:

The Prince of the Mohoks knew me again perfectly weel I being often in his company at Lond° in Queen Anns time. . . . He is now a Polite Gentleman Baptized, a Zealous Christian apparell^d as we, Speaks pretty good English and Scarsely distinguishable from an Englishman but by his tawny complexion, when he came to known my designe, he Invited me very lovingly up to his Country & Spoke to the Rest of the Princes to the same purpose who all very willingly did the same. . . .

More accepted the royal invitation. Some months later Sherard informed his fellow scientist, Richard Richardson:

THE KING OF THE RIVER NATION

Painted by John Verelst
Engraved by John Simon

'I have heard nothing yet from the Pilgrim Botanist, which I admire at. Col. Dudley wrote word he was gone up into the country, to visit his old acquaintance the Indian Kings that were in England. I had rather he would first send what grows near Boston; but they have all the notion that, the further they go, the more rare things they find.'

These 'petty Kings', travelling from the Mohawk to the Thames and back once more to their own Indian castles, had themselves gone far and found rare things, and if Mr. More joined his friends, they doubtless gave a fair reward to his journey and guided him to good hunting among the flora of their great wilderness.

III

Art and Letters

WHILE the four Kings from America were seeing London for a short month in the spring of 1710, they were themselves a sight for thousands of Londoners. The man in the street could watch the savage envoys ride to their appointments; the person of quality could have better view of the ambassadors extraordinary at some select place of attendance; and the hunters after current celebrities could crowd into the assemblies announced for the entertainment of the foreign princes. This curiosity and excitement over the sachems made London a wide market for special tokens of the Mohawks—a broadside poem in their honour, a pamphlet on life in their far kingdom, a mezzotint from portraits by skilful painters. Almost anything would do, trivial or expert, so long as it memorialized the interest of that hour, and for this sudden trade versifier, proseman, and engraver quickly collaborated with publisher to fill London's need. The sailing of the sachems gave no prompt stay to separate publications concerning them; and in time they became matter for casual topical reference in prose and verse, and even a subject for consideration by the great Mr. Spectator.

First, the pictures of the Kings. The most elaborate and famous were whole-length portraits by John Verelst, who was alleged to have the sole liberty to take them and even the Kings' certificate attesting the truth of this unique privilege. The Queen paid Verelst £100, plus 'Office ffees', for the four paintings, which were seen in October of 1710 by the German traveller von Uffenbach in a small room at Kensington Palace.

Even before the Kings left Plymouth an anonymous

craftsman produced a print called *The true Effiges of the Four Indian Kings taken from the Original Paintings done by M^r. Varelst*. Four oval bust drawings of the Indians are grouped around their totem marks, 'Coats of Arms which they Use instead of signing their Names'. John Morphew announced in his semi-weekly paper, the *Supplement*, that the likenesses on this sheet were engraved on copper and that 'all others are only Counterfeits, done by Guess, on old Plates', but these pictures differ from the portraits by Verelst in so many ways that they could rightly have no title as true copies of his work. Indeed, the next day among the advertisements in the *Tatler*, sold only by the same Morphew, appeared a denial by Verelst himself, saying that he had permitted no draft or sketch to be made from his paintings and that 'If he should, he would take Care to have it correctly done by a skilful Hand, and inform the Publick thereof in the Tatler.'

Verelst proceeded as he promised—in due time he informed the public through repeated notices in the *Tatler* that he had allowed drafts of his portraits to be taken by a skilful hand, that of John Simon, a well-established Huguenot engraver. In these four authorized engravings each King stands facing front, one hand on hip, with a robe over his shoulders and at his feet a tomahawk and the animal of his clan. Emperor Hendrick alone wears European habit and holds an unmartial belt of wampum in a peaceful forest. The others are attired less formally and are heavily marked, have ear ornaments and moccasins, and carry weapons, with a fight or a hunt in the forest behind them. All the details of the portraits—the rich costumes and settings, the robust figures, the alert faces—combine to give an impression of mature poise and sensible strength proper to leaders of a savage ally. Such true effigies at once attained, and long maintained, the largest popularity among the mezzotints printed to 'make a shew' of the Kings.

On 2 May Bernard Lens, third of that name, painted miniature portraits of the Indians on ivory; in fact, Lens painted two sets of miniatures, perhaps for different clients. The sachems are all dressed alike, with red ear ornaments, white shirts, black coats, and scarlet cloaks, but in their golden brown faces it is easy to discover the individuality of the four men. These oval busts were reproduced by the artist's father on one sheet, 'Done after the Original Limnings Drawn from ye Life by B. Lens jun^r.' The Emperor holds the favoured position on the print. His face alone is unmarked; the others are all ornamented, Brant most of all, with face, neck, and chest splendidly adorned with designs. Each mezzotint is surrounded by an elaborate frame topped by a crown of five feathers and crossed Indian weapons (different for each warrior), and each monarch is identified below his engraving by name and title. This print presents the only worthy cluster of the Kings.

A third set of portraits was 'Done from ye Life' by John Faber the elder, also in oval busts. Faber moreover 'Fecit & Excudt' the mezzotints, and concluded the operation by selling the prints at his own shop near the Savoy, an opportunity shared by J. King in the Poultry. In these engravings all four figures wear shirts with cloaks loosely draped around their shoulders; Hendrick has no ear ornaments or face markings, and he looks to be the oldest, saddest, and wisest. Faber's engravings travelled to Amsterdam, where the German artist Peter Schenck copied them and issued the set in reverse (an easier process than redrawing) with legends partly in Dutch.

To still another set of images was joined a piece of verse in a collaboration of inadequacy. Four small oval portraits 'taken from the Life and Curiously Engrav'd' by Sutton Nicholls, who also sold this catchpenny labour, offer small differentiation among the monarchs in face and raiment; quite probably the artist had no artistic audience of the sachems and so produced a stereotype. The lower half of the sheet, to justify its title of *The Four Indian Kings Speech*, presents the gist of their address to the Queen 'Translated into verse by T. S.'. In the two dozen couplets of thin gruel warmed over, the middle is as good as the beginning or the end:

> Then Long we waited for the English Fleet
> At who's arival *Victory* more compleat
> Than ever yet By Art or Arms was Gain'd
> We do perswade our Selves had been obtain'd
> But being disapointed for that Season
> By bus'nes of Import our Great Queens Reason
> Extreamly Sorrowfull it did *us* make.

The makers of ballads delayed not to give voice. A collection of ditties called *Three Ballads Concerning the Times*, 'Which may be sung or said by either the Nobility, Gentility, or Mobility, both Male and Female. To the Tune of, *A Soldier and a Sailor*, &c.' was offered for a penny by John Baker, who also sold Defoe's *Review* at his Black Boy in Paternoster Row. Therein appeared 'The Royal Embassy', subtitled 'A Ballad on the Progress of the four Indian Kings, that have come so many thousand Leagues to see her present Majesty.'

> FOUR Kings, each God's Vicegerent,
> With Right divine inherent,
> Have lately cross'd the Main, Sir,
> An Audience to gain, Sir,
>   Of *Britain*'s Empress *Anne*.
> Which she has kindly granted,
> To know what Aids they wanted,
> By giving each an Answer,
> When they had kiss'd her Hand, Sir,
>   As pleas'd 'em ev'ry Man.

The lines say little fast enough, and the poem as a whole fulfils the requisites of ephemera.

Another exercise in versification, done by a Person of Quality and published in 1710 by W. Wise in Fetter Lane, Fleet Street, bears the title of *The Royal Strangers Ramble*, expanded into 'The Remarkable Lives, Customs, and Character of the Four Indian Kings: With the manner of their Daily Pastimes, Humours and Behaviours since their first landing in England. Render'd into Pleasant and Familiar Verse.'

> Four Monarchs of Worth,
> From their Kingdoms set forth,
>   Without Hose or Shoes to their Feet;
> In order to know
> How Affairs did here go,
>   And of Things of Importance to Treat.

The dozen dozen lines, less pleasant than familiar, though they do not justify the breadth of their sub-title, contain more information on the actual movements of the Kings than does any other contemporary piece of verse, so that the reportorial value of this broadside almost compensates for the crudity of its inditement. But the *Ramble* ends less factually than was warranted, and with more gloom:

> Since no one brought less
> Of Wealth, Knowledge and Dress
>   Than these who from *India* are come,
> And no one before
> Return'd from our Shore
>   With so little Advantages Home.

A third ballad, *The Four Indian Kings*, is bad, but better. This royal rhyme has two parts—'How a beautiful Lady conquered one of the Indian Kings' and 'The Lady's Answer to the Indian King's Request'. After presenting the monarchs to the English courts, the balladist introduces the romance.

> With a glance of Britain's glory,
>   Buildings, troops, & many things,
> But now comes a pressing story,
>   Love seiz'd one of these four kings.

It happened in St. James's Park, where 'waited Troops of handsome ladies fair', and the youngest of these Kings is smitten at sight. Straightway he laments:

> But I fear she cannot love me,
>   I must hope for no such thing:
> That sweet saint is far above me,
>   Altho' I am an Indian King.

Before dying a martyr to love, he instructs an envoy to bear her his royal token of a diamond ring, with a plea for a quick answer, each minute of delay seeming an hour and each hour seeming six. The messenger is to stress the lady's power to kill or cure speedily, and should seek her Christian charity for one 'Wrapt in scorching flame of love'.

In Part II the King's courier flies with his petition, after hoping that the lady would be endowed with reason so that labour would be not spent in vain. He presents the diamond and the message. The lady is sorry, but she will never 'wed a Heathen, For the richest Indian shore'. The spokesman for love tries again, recalling of the King and his colleagues

> How well they lik'd this place;
> And declar'd themselves right wiling
>   To receive the light of grace.

Thus he pleads,

> Quench the flame, abate the fuel,
>   Spare his life to save his soul.

She listens, and sends her final answer:

> Tell your master this for me,
> Let him, let him first be turned,
> From his gross idolatry.
> If he will become a Christian,
>   Live up to the truth reveal'd,
> I will make him grant the question
>   Or before wi'l never yield.
> Altho' he was pleas'd to send to me,
>   His fine ring and diamond stone,
> With this answer pray comend me
>   To your master yet unknown.

Here ends the first version, a sad sooth of religion versus love and the triumph of the former. But a happy conclusion was later added wherein are reconciled love sacred and love profane—in a few lines the King turns Christian, the lady of quality accepts him, and the Queen honours the wedding with the Royal Presence.

This story of high life and quick love between a very affectionate sovereign and a very beautiful lady became one of the most popular ballads of the eighteenth century and survived into the next. At least fifteen different printings have been preserved, eleven of the short version and four of the longer. Six of the fifteen were called 'garlands', two of which, incidentally, reduce the number of Kings to three. The year of publication is not stated on any of them, probably to prevent outdating, nor is the place of publication given in each case. London presumably fathered the majority, but printers in Tewkesbury, Worcester, Hull, Coventry, and Gateshead, and possibly in Newcastle and Whitehaven, issued their own editions. The favourite formats were the folio broadside and the short pamphlet. The invitation to embellish the text with a woodcut was met by most of the printers with ornaments typical of broadside variety—a ship; a man's head; one King, both head and full length; three Kings,

robed, sceptred, and crowned, with and without a lady;
busts of four Kings, also conventional. J. Ferraby of Hull
issued the 'garland' once with a cut of a stationary lady
and gentleman and again with the gentleman mildly pur-
suing his inamorata. One woodcut actually portrayed
Indians. And J. Pitts of Great St. Andrew Street, to
illustrate his text of *The Four Indian Kings*, found in his
box only a cut of the Three Wise Men and the Star of
Bethlehem, and with it he made a meeting of East and
West perchance better than he knew. So much for the
balladeers.

In 1711 Elkanah Settle produced a chauvinistic *Pindaric Poem, on the Propagation of the Gospel in Foreign Parts*.
In his prefatory address to the Queen, Settle compares
the work of the Society to that of the Crusades, the former
proving less hazardous but more important in the aboli-
tion of infidelity. He cites the 'Royal Suppliants, the late
Indian Princes, brought over in their naked Simplicity and
uncultivated Innocence' to praise the methods of British
missions:

So happy these Honour'd *Americans* from the Reception of
such generous *European Visitants* amongst them, beyond their
once more hard-fated *Indian Neighbours* when first visited by
the barbarous *Spaniard*. Yes the Benign BRITANNIA to
the Immortal Honour of her *Sovereign MISTRESS* sends no
Cortesian Tyrants, no *Bloody Streamers* to hang out amongst
them. Ah no, our *British Voyagers* carry not only the *Flag*,
but *GOD* of *PEACE* along with them.

Settle had been appointed City Poet, and here he gains
citation as imperial Laureate of the pious line.

> And now, my Muse, *America* survey,
> You'll find the Phosphor of advancing Day
> In our Plantations gratefully arise
> And Jesus dawning thro the *Indian* Skyes.
> The *English* Miter sent it's Envoys there
> To chase the Vapours from that Cloudy Sphere,

And the exterminated Shades supply
With the bright Aspect of the *British* Sky.
See there their *Indian* Majesties on Knees
Waiting for Heav'ns, & Royal *Anne*'s Decrees:
The swarthy Monarchs, negligent of Gold,
 And trifling Gems, & whatsoe'er
  We Christians hold so Dear,
And with devouring Eyes, and captive Hearts behold,
 Look above Mines, & what the Mines produce
 For Treasure of a more exalted Use,
  For Light to shew the Heav'nly Way,
  And guide 'em with a friendly Ray
Where the Road leads to Everlasting Day.

Two years later the first poet of Anne's reign, Alexander
Pope, also chose to celebrate the relation of Her Majesty
to suppliant royalty. During the visit of the sachems the
young poet was living at Binfield, and could have seen
them in London; certainly he would have been strangely
out of touch with metropolitan matters not to be aware
of their presence. To honour the Tory Peace of Utrecht
he in 1713 revised some sylvan verses for publication as
Windsor-Forest. Therein Father Thames proclaims the
glories of Anne, Windsor, peace, and prosperity; looking
into the future, Pope saw the grandeur of a regal reception suggested, like enough, by the visit of the four
Kings.

There mighty Nations shall inquire their Doom,
The World's great Oracle in Times to come;
There Kings shall sue, and suppliant States be seen
Once more to bend before a *British* QUEEN. . . .
The Time shall come, when free as Seas or Wind
Unbounded *Thames* shall flow for all Mankind,
Whole Nations enter with each swelling Tyde,
And Oceans join whom they did first divide;
Earth's distant Ends our Glory shall behold,
And the new World launch forth to seek the Old.

Then Ships of uncouth Form shall stem the Tyde,
And Feather'd People crowd my wealthy Side,
And naked Youth and painted Chiefs admire
Our Speech, our Colour, and our strange Attire!

Pope, to be sure, does not directly allude to the four Indian Kings, but their visit to Windsor and the poet's acquaintance with current events advance the probability that he was indirectly referring to them or at least using a half-memory of them.

Daniel Defoe was more explicit. He did not ever write the surprising adventures of these Kings in strange lands and seas, but he could hardly omit them from his omnivorous journal of commentary on current affairs, well styled *A Review of the State of the British Nation*. His first reference appeared in August of 1710, a month of national crisis and a time when the Tories in their new success would favour the exercise of public spirit by the Whigs, especially since public credit had declined at the change of government. Defoe appealed to the Whigs, no longer at the helm, to hand the sails of the ship of state, heave the lead, and work the pumps, since all 'must Sink and Swim together'. And to illustrate his belief in such national principles he chose far outlanders in the East and the West:

I know not *who*, or *what* they are, her Majesty *has* or *will*, put in to Trust, I am not talking of Persons, or of Parties, here——But if the Grand Seigneur's *Mufty* were to come hither, and be Prime Minister; If the four *Indian* Salvages, *we call'd Kings*, were to be Commissioners; yet if these applied themselves diligently, and faithfully, to carry on the War, support the Confederacy, oppose *France*, and defend us against the Pretender, God forbid any *Whigg* should be found, that would not join with them, *because he did not like the Men*; no, no, Gentlemen, the Nation must not *be given up to France*, the *Jacobites* must not have their Ends of us *so*.

Defoe's later and larger reference to the Kings grew

from the current excitement over the Mohocks, the rake-hells who in their drunken sallies on the Town scoured the watch, tormented and tortured unarmed citizens, and generally indulged their sense of physical humour. They gained record in letters, diaries, broadsides, and gazettes, and entered literature by way of the *Spectator* and John Gay's poem *Trivia* and farce *The Mohocks*. Among these vicious pranksters Whigs and Tories identified each other as makers of a plot; some observers discounted the Mohock violence and even the existence of such a club, and others exaggerated. The name itself was certainly derived from that of the Indians who less than two years earlier had shown their savage selves in London and who represented a people long supposed to delight in savage ways. Innocently enough the Mohawk sachems offered a convenient name for these 'Kindlers of riot.'

> Who has not heard the *Scowrer*'s midnight fame?
> Who has not trembled at the *Mohock*'s name?

The Kings, belike, never learned of this stain on their English scutcheon, and seldom were the sachems themselves or their nation mentioned during the months of Mohock sport as furnishing the parent term, but Defoe made its derivation sharply clear. On 12 March 1712 the *Spectator* published the letter of 'Philanthropos' concerning the Mohock Club, bearing 'a Name borrowed it seems from a sort of *Cannibals* in *India*, who subsist by plundering and devouring all the Nations about them'. Without marking that this offending passage was not by Mr. Spectator but by one of his correspondents, Defoe in the *Review* promptly entered his dissent, along with an opinion on the errand of the Kings perhaps darkened by political ink.

With Submission to the Ingenious *Spectator*, I must dissent from his Opinion, That the *Mohocks*, from whence these People are Sir-nam'd, are a People of *India*, tho' the End of the Argument is the same; the *Mohock*, or *Mowhawks*, are, or rather were, *for they are Extinct now, or very near it*, a small Nation of *Savages* in the Woods, on the back of our two Colonies of *New-England* and *New York*, the same from whence our four pretended *Indian* Kings came lately of their own Fools Errand; they were always esteem'd as the most Desperate, and most Cruel of the Natives of *North-America*; and it was a particular Barbarity singular to them, that when they took any Prisoners, either of the *English* or other Natives, they always *Scalp'd them*, as they call'd it, *viz*. pared the Skin and Hair off from the Crown of their Heads, and so left the Body to lie and Languish without any pity, till it died—With several other Barbarities peculiar to themselves, which many of our poor *English* People have felt, when they had the Misfortune to fall into their Hands.

The prose journeymen of 1710 quickly exacted tribute from the popular excitement over the Kings with three anonymous tracts for the times. One of these, graciously brief, was *The History and Progress of the four Indian Kings*, an ill-printed pamphlet with the figures of four crowned, un-Indian monarchs on the title-page. After explaining the presence of the Iroquois in England, the pamphleteer spends half his strength on the marital customs of the Americans and the other on miscellaneous manners. His comments on the art of trade and science of language illustrate his contribution to knowledge:

The Women here are tolerably Handsome, at least our *English* Traders don't stick to think 'em so, for they are seldom without an *Indian* Female for a Bed-fellow, alledging these Reasons, as sufficient to allow of this Familiarity. *First*, That these Indians being remote from white People, it helps to preserve their Friendship with 'em, they esteeming a White Man's Child, much above one of their own getting; the *Indian* Mistriss ever securing her White Friend whilst he stays amongst them; and also, that this Correspondence makes 'em learn the *Indian* Tongue with more facility, they being of the *French* Man's Opinion, that an English Wife teaches her Husband more English in one Night, than a School-master can do in a Week.

The speech to the Queen is then reprinted, together with half the Haymarket epilogue to fill the final page.

A second tract, called *The History of the Four Indian Kings*, reserved for the end its pictorial embellishment, a cut of the four Kings as they prostrate themselves before Her Majesty. This 'history' opens with a thirty-nine-line sentence, indulges in fulsome compliments to Anne and Christendom, reveals nothing about the sachems beyond their names, and closes with their address to the Queen remodelled into inexcusable couplets.

The third pamphlet is an improvement in style and contents—*The Four Kings of Canada*. An introductory chapter provides a description of the Kings and reprints their address to the Queen. The remaining fourteen sections correspond to the summary on the title-page:

A particular Description of their Country, their strange and remarkable Religion, Feasts, Marriages, Burials, Remedies for their Sick, Customs, Manners, Constitution, Habits, Sports, War, Peace, Policy, Hunting, Fishing, Utensils belonging to the Savages, with several other Extraordinary Things worthy Observation, as to the natural or curious Productions, Beauty, or Fertility, of that Part of the World.

This 'Succinct Account' is as a whole a capable tract of its kind, meaning that its information on Indian life is the mixture of fact, fancy, and tradition which a busy scissors-and-paster would be able to make from such a work as the Baron de Lahontan's *New Voyages to North-America* of 1703.

The intelligent reader during the latter half of Anne's reign could often, by passing from pamphlet to essay periodical, exchange the timely for the timeless. And so it was in the matter of the red men. The difference between the occasional tracts on the Kings and the columns in the *Tatler* and *Spectator* on their visit is the difference between letterpress and literature. On Saturday, 13 May 1710, while the Kings waited at Plymouth for favourable

winds, Steele in his *Tatler* No. 171 employed the Indians
to illustrate his witty lucubration on titles of honour and
the man of contradiction expert also in 'secret history'.
The taste of Mr. Bickerstaff for the contemporary ex-
tended beyond the late residence of the Kings in King
Street to include the fact that one of them had lost,
through illness, several days of their public pastime. He
reported thus from the Grecian Coffee-house.

It has happened to be for some Days the Deliberation of the
Learnedest Board in this House, whence Honour and Title
had its first Original. *Timoleon,* who is very particular in his
Opinions, but is thought particular for no other Cause but that
he acts against depraved Custom, by the Rules of Nature and
Reason, in a very handsome Discourse gave the Company to
understand, That in those Ages which first degenerated from
Simplicity of Life, and Natural Justice, the Wise among them
thought it necessary to inspire Men with the Love of Virtue,
by giving them who adhered to the Interests of Innocence and
Truth, some distinguishing Name to raise them above the
common Level of Mankind. This Way of fixing Appellations
of Credit upon eminent Merit, was what gave Being to Titles
and Terms of Honour. Such a Name, continued he, without
the Qualities which should give a Man Pretence to be exalted
above others, does but turn him to Jest and Ridicule. Should
one see another cudgelled, or scurvily treated, Do you think a
Man so used would take it kindly to be called *Hector,* or
Alexander? Every Thing must bear a Proportion with the
outward Value that is set upon it; or instead of being long had
in Veneration, that very Term of Esteem will become a Word
of Reproach. When *Timoleon* had done speaking, *Urbanus* pursued the same Purpose, by giving an Account of the Manner
in which the *Indian* Kings who were lately in *Great Britain,* did
Honour to the Person where they lodged. They were placed,
said he, in an handsom Apartment, at an Upholsterers in *King-
street, Covent-Garden.* The Man of the House, it seems, had been
very observant of them, and ready in their Service. These just
and generous Princes, who act according to the Dictates of
natural Justice, thought it proper to confer some Dignity

upon their Landlord before they left his House. One of them had been sick during his Residence there, and having never before been in a Bed, had a very great Veneration for him who made that Engine of Repose, so useful and so necessary in his Distress. It was consulted among the Four Princes, by what Name to dignify his great Merit and Services. The Emperor of the *Mohocks*, and the other Three Kings, stood up, and in that Posture recounted the Civilities they had received, and particularly repeated the Care which was taken of their Sick Brother. This, in their Imagination, who are used to know the Injuries of Weather, and the Vicissitudes of Cold and Heat, gave them very great Impressions of a skilful Upholsterer, whose Furniture was so well contrived for their Protection on such Occasions. It is with these less instructed (I will not say less knowing) People, the Manner of doing Honour, to impose some Name significant of the Qualities of the Person they distinguish, and the good Offices received from him. It was therefore resolved, to call their Landlord *Cadaroque*, which is the Name of the strongest Fort in their Part of the World. When they had agreed upon the Name, they sent for their Landlord, and as he entered into their Presence, the Emperor of the *Mohocks* taking him by the Hand, called him *Cadoroque*. After which the other Three Princes repeated the same Word and Ceremony.

Timoleon appeared much satisfied with this Account, and having a Philosophick Turn, began to argue against the Modes and Manners of those Nations which we esteem polite, and express himself with Disdain at our usual Method of calling such as are Strangers to our Innovations, barbarous. I have, says he, so great a Deference for the Distinction given by these Princes, that *Cadaroque* shall be my Upholsterer. He was going on, but the intended Discourse was interrupted by *Minucius*, who sat near him, a small Philosopher, who is also somewhat of a Politician; one of those who set up for Knowledge by Doubting, and has no other Way of making himself considerable but by contradicting all he hears said. He has, besides much Doubt and a Spirit of Contradiction, a constant Suspicion as to State-Affairs. This accomplish'd Gentleman, with a very awful Brow, and a Countenance full of Weight, told *Timoleon*,

THE EMPEROR OF THE SIX NATIONS
Painted and Engraved by John Faber

That it was a great Misfortune Men of Letters seldom looked into the Bottom of Things. Will any Man, continued he, perswade me, that this was not from the Beginning to the End a concerted Affair? Who can convince the World, that Four Kings shall come over here, and lie at the Two Crowns and Cushion, and one of them fall sick, and the Place be called *King-street*, and all this by meer Accident? No, no: To a Man of very small Penetration, it appears, that *Tee Yee Neen Ho Ga Row*, Emperor of the *Mohocks*, was prepared for this Adventure before-hand. I do not care to contradict any Gentleman in his Discourse; but I may say, however *Sa Ga Yeath Rua Geth Ton*, and *E Tow Oh Koam*, might be surprised in this Matter; nevertheless, *Ho Nec Yeth Taw No Row*, knew it before he set Foot on the *English* Shore.

On 27 April 1711, almost a year after the Kings had left the 'Two Crowns', a new periodical named the *Spectator* printed an essay written as if by one of 'this little Fraternity of Kings'. It was the fiftieth issue of the daily sheet and the thirtieth contribution by Mr. Addison. Behind the character mask of the worthy Mr. Spectator Addison utilizes the pseudo-journal of a foreign observer to reprove such English readers as might not heed the words of their own countryman—a technique later called, in honour of its use by Goldsmith, the citizen-of-the-world device. By such indirection, observations and experiences which at first seem naïve turn on second thought into sophisticated comments, and the perceptiveness of the reader is enhanced, and thus also his pleasure in the essay.

When the four *Indian* Kings were in this Country about a Twelve-month ago, I often mix'd with the Rabble and followed them a whole Day together, being wonderfully struck with the Sight of every thing that is new or uncommon. I have, since their Departure, employed a Friend to make many Enquiries of their Landlord the Upholsterer relating to their Manners and Conversation, as also concerning the Remarks which they made in this Country: For next to the forming a right Notion of such Strangers, I should be desirous of learning what Ideas they have conceived of us.

The Upholsterer finding my Friend very inquisitive about these his Lodgers, brought him some time since a little Bundle of Papers, which he assured him were written by King *Sa Ga Yean Qua Rash Tow*, and, as he supposes, left behind by some Mistake. These Papers are now translated, and contain abundance of very odd Observations, which I find this little Fraternity of Kings made during their Stay in the Isle of *Great Britain*. I shall present my Reader with a short Specimen of them in this Paper, and may perhaps communicate more to him hereafter. In the Article of *London* are the following Words, which without Doubt are meant of the Church of St. *Paul*.

'On the most rising Part of the Town there stands a huge House, big enough to contain the whole Nation of which I am King. Our good Brother *E Tow O Koam* King of the *Rivers*, is of Opinion it was made by the Hands of that great God to whom it is consecrated. The Kings of *Granajah* and of the *Six Nations* believe that it was created with the Earth, and produced on the same Day with the Sun and Moon. But for my own Part, by the best Information that I could get of this Matter, I am apt to think that this prodigious Pile was fashioned into the Shape it now bears by several Tools and Instruments, of which they have a wonderful Variety in this Country. It was probably at first an huge mis-shapen Rock that grew upon the Top of the Hill, which the Natives of the Country (after having cut it into a kind of regular Figure) bored and hollowed with incredible Pains and Industry, till they had wrought in it all those beautiful Vaults and Caverns into which it is divided at this Day. As soon as this Rock was thus curiously scooped to their Liking, a prodigious Number of Hands must have been employed in chipping the Outside of it, which is now as smooth as polished Marble; and is in several Places hewn out into Pillars that stand like the Trunks of so many Trees bound about the Top with Garlands of Leaves. It is probable that when this great Work was begun, which must have been many Hundred Years ago, there was some Religion among this People; for they give it the Name of a Temple, and have a Tradition that it was designed for Men to pay their Devotions in. And indeed, there are several Reasons which make us think, that the Natives of this Country had formerly among them some sort of Worship; for they set apart every seventh Day as sacred: But upon my going into one of those holy Houses on that Day, I could not observe any Circumstance of Devotion in their Behaviour: There was indeed a Man in Black who was mounted above the rest, and seemed to utter something with a great deal of Vehemence; but as for those underneath him, instead of paying their Worship to the Deity of the Place, they were most of them bowing and curtisying to one another, and a considerable Number of them fast asleep.

'The Queen of the Country appointed two Men to attend us, that had enough of our Language to make themselves understood in some few Particulars. But we soon perceived these two were great Enemies to one another, and did not always agree in the same Story. We could make a Shift to gather out of one of them, that this Island was very much infested with a monstrous Kind of Animals, in the Shape of Men, called *Whigs*; and he often told us, that he hoped we should meet with none of them in our Way, for that if we did, they would be apt to knock us down for being Kings.

'Our other Interpreter used to talk very much of a kind of Animal called a *Tory*, that was as great a Monster as the *Whig*, and would treat us as ill for being Foreigners. These two Creatures, it seems, are born with a secret Antipathy to one another, and engage when they meet as naturally as the Elephant and the Rhinoceros. But as we saw none of either of these Species, we are apt to think that our Guides deceived us with Misrepresentations and Fictions, and amused us with an Account of such Monsters as are not really in their Country.

'These Particulars we made Shift to pick out from the Discourse of our Interpreters; which we put together as well as we could, being able to understand but here and there a Word of what they said, and afterwards making up the Meaning of it among our selves. The Men of the Country are very cunning and ingenious in handicraft Works; but withal so very idle, that we often saw young lusty raw-boned Fellows carried up and down the Streets in little covered Rooms by a Couple of Porters who are hired for that Service. Their Dress is likewise very barbarous, for they almost strangle themselves about the Neck, and bind their Bodies with many Ligatures, that we are apt to think are the Occasion of several Distempers among them which our Country is entirely free from. Instead of those beautiful Feathers with which we adorn our Heads, they often buy up a monstrous Bush of Hair, which covers their Heads, and falls down in a large Fleece below the Middle of their Backs; with which they walk up and down the Streets, and are as proud of it as if it was of their own Growth.

'We were invited to one of their publick Diversions, where we hoped to have seen the great Men of their Country running down a Stag or pitching a Bar, that we might have discover'd who were the Men of the greatest Perfections in their Country; but instead of that, they conveyed us into an huge Room lighted up with abundance of Candles, where this lazy People sat still above three Hours to see several Feats of Ingenuity performed by others, who it seems were paid for it.

'As for the Women of the Country, not being able to talk with them, we could only make our Remarks upon them at a Distance. They let the Hair of their Heads grow to a great Length; but as the Men make a great Show with Heads of Hair that are none of their own, the Women, who they say have very fine Heads of Hair, tie it up in a Knot and cover it from being seen. The Women look like Angels, and would be more beautiful than the Sun, were it not for little black Spots that are apt to break out in their Faces, and sometimes rise in very odd Figures. I have observed that those little Blemishes wear off very soon; but when they disappear in one Part of the Face, they are very apt to break out in another, insomuch that I have seen a Spot upon the Forehead in the Afternoon, which was upon the Chin in the Morning.'

The Author then proceeds to shew the Absurdity of Breeches and Petticoats, with many other curious Observations, which I shall reserve for another Occasion. I cannot however conclude this Paper without taking Notice, That amidst these wild Remarks there now and then appears something very reasonable. I can't likewise forbear observing, That we are all guilty in some Measure of the same narrow Way of Thinking which we meet with in this Abstract of the *Indian* Journal; when we

fancy the Customs, Dresses, and Manners of other Countries
are ridiculous and extravagant, if they do not resemble those of
our own.

So through the sachems, who had asked for missionaries to their people, comes reproach of Englishmen's
indifference to religion; and through Indians, too often
deployed for the ends of party war, comes comment on
such warfare. Best of all, here is a prose style with matter
married to its proper manner, the pattern for pens that
venture familiar eloquence.

On the morning after the appearance of Addison's
'Abstract of the *Indian* Journal' Jonathan Swift wrote
about it in his journal to Stella:

The *Spectator* is written by Steele, with Addison's help: 'tis
often very pretty. Yesterday it was made of a noble hint I
gave him long ago for his *Tatlers*, about an Indian supposed
to write his travels into England. I repent he ever had it. I
intended to have written a book on that subject. I believe he
has spent it all in one paper, and all the under-hints there are
mine too; but I never see him or Addison.

The tone of irritation is audible enough: Swift and his
old Whig friends had already begun to cool their friendship, and by his papers in the Tory *Examiner* he had
become a rival journalist. He erred, pardonably, in attri-
buting the *Spectator* essay to Steele, who had apparently
passed the hint to Addison. Less pardonable was his
easy abandonment of a possibly powerful work after the
publication of one short essay, which he had himself
suggested and which had far from 'spent it all'. Perhaps
in his statement of intention Cousin Jonathan was merely
indulging his own foolery or his own spleen. Was this
book of Swift's related to the treatise he had seven years
earlier lightly announced as speedily to be published—
'*A Voyage into* England, *by a Person of Quality in* Terra
Australis incognita, *translated from the Original*'? And

was this projected book of travels into England by an Indian itself the noble hint for the sovereign book of travels by a worthy English surgeon-mariner out of the known world into the fabulous and back again? Whatever the answers, Swift suggested the best excursion the Indian Kings made into English literature.

The next day a reader of the *Spectator* signing himself J. H. was moved to write a letter to the editor about the Indian's journal. Despite his esteem for Mr. Spectator and his writings J. H. could not patiently 'see the laws of hospitality violated, and her majesties allies traduced'. He begins his protest: 'I am indeed, no great traveller; but I have read here and there an odd book, ran through many prefaces and tables: all which, has enabled me so far to commence a critick, that I almost dare be positive, the memoirs you are pleased to father on the four Indian kings, are no more genuine than those that go under the name of the Turkish spy.' First, continues J. H., it is not probable that those monarchs could write at all, but he will let that pass. Next, it seems unlikely that Indians would be ignorant of the possibility of raising a building with stones and yet be so well acquainted with polished marble, or that the Kings could not distinguish between the smoothness of marble and that of Portland stone. Still more improbable is it that appointed cicerones would be so impolitic as to expose 'the weak side of our constitution' at such a critical juncture, and it is a question whether the Whigs and Tories should be presented in terms of four-legged beasts.

This is no more likely than that these royal travellers should compare them to the great elephant and the rhinoceros. In some mapps of Africa and the East-indies, these animals are indeed pretty frequent, and sometimes of an excessive bulk. I remember to have seen an elephant situated to the south-west of the mountains of the Moon, whose body, without including trunk or legs, was nine degrees and seventeen minutes in length, and five degrees and half in breadth; and almost bordering upon him was a rhinoceros, who by the extent of his frontiers seemed very near as formidable; but it never was my luck to meet with either of these big or little in a map of North-America.

This letter did not appear in the *Spectator*, but remained unprinted until the publication, fourteen years later, of a large number of letters originally sent to but discarded by the *Tatler* and *Spectator*. It is plausible that Steele hesitated to accept it for publication from an uncertainty whether J. H. was sincerely applying an artless realism to the feigned journal by a foreign visitor or was attempting to advance the literary device with an artful sobriety.

The readers of *Spectator* No. 50 received hope of further remarks by the Indian author on another occasion. But Mr. Spectator did not allow himself the privilege or requirement of fulfilling all his journalistic pledges: no second instalment of the 'recovered' papers of the sachem appeared. However, one week later, in No. 56, Addison returned to the Kings in an essay on the souls of departed things and creatures. He refers to a 'Tradition among the *Americans*' that in a vision one of them descended to the regions of the dead and on his return gave an account of all he saw. 'A Friend of mine, whom I have formerly mentioned, prevailed upon one of the Interpreters of the *Indian* Kings, to enquire of them, if possible, what Tradition they have among them of this Matter: Which, as well as he could learn by those many Questions which he asked them at several Times, was in Substance as follows.' An account is then given of the chimerical journey by an Indian named Marraton from the land of the living to the world of happy spirits and his meeting there with his wife and children. Addison not infrequently selected the vision as fictional form, and in this essay he used the visiting sachems as a natural medium for transmitting the vision, a form better for such an incorporeal subject than a continuation of the satiric pseudo-journal of the King of the Maquas.

Two decades after Mr. Spectator had presented his short specimen of the 'very odd Observations' in the bundle of Indian papers, an anonymous satirist foisted his own wares on the Mohawk King in a work he entitled *Royal Remarks; or, the Indian King's Observations On the most Fashionable Follies: Now reigning in the Kingdom of Great-Britain*. He opens his discourse with the first sentences of the *Spectator* essay and then, abandoning both the King (renamed Ouka) and Mr. Spectator's point of view, worries the theme of etymology, with constant undertones of the times, through the characters of Squire Wronghead, Doctor Puzzlepate, and Will Blunderbuss. To read these fifty-five pages of dim, dull words signifying next to nothing becomes a task of pointless penance, and quotation would be imposition. It is just and kind to restore the *Royal Remarks* to its seat in scarce obscurity.

The fame of the *Spectator* essay on the sachems was revived with dignity in 1742 by its namesake, *The Universal Spectator, and Weekly Journal*, an essay-newspaper 'By Henry Stonecastle, of Lincoln's-Inn, Esq;' né Henry Baker. After lamenting that his 'Predecessor did not deliver down to us the remaining Part of the Manuscript of that Serene Monarch, *Sa Ga Yern Qua Rash Tow*, one of the *Indian Kings*, who was here in the Reign of Queen *Anne*', Mr. Stonecastle offers on successive Saturdays two essays which give his Indian Majesty's comments as faithfully rendered from a manuscript in the possession of an obliging correspondent. This double essay mocks vice and folly in general, with a special application to dicing, masquerades, the playhouse and opera, beaux and coquettes, coffee-houses, the law, and the Exchange. The editor himself commends this 'Voice of Nature and Reason' and anticipates the shocked objections of the

Fair. '*Cleora*, I don't doubt, will give herself abundance of Airs upon this Occasion, and frequently cry out, with a pretty Shriek, *Ah! odious, abominable Savage! hideous, hideous* Indian! *&c.* But I wish the dear Creature would reflect a little seriously, view herself in the Glass he presents, and discover her own Likeness in the Picture he draws of *Affectation.* . . .'

In 1762 another Indian King, Ostenaco of the Cherokees, with two attendant sachems, visited England, and another document in the *Spectator* lineage was 'found' among the loose papers of a visiting prince and was 'translated' by the very interpreter to the chiefs 'that were over here about thirty years ago'. While these guests were heartily accepting the freedom of London, there appeared in the *St. James's Chronicle; or, the British Evening-Post* a letter as from Tohanohawighton, the 'Great Warrior', to Yasoma, Commander of the Cherokees in his absence. The visitor, who has already sent an account of the delegation's reception, now confesses to a desire to pass a considerable portion of his life in England 'as the English are, beyond Dispute, a brave People, though undoubtedly inferior to the Cherokee Nation, and tinctured with many Follies which we are entirely free from'. These follies he promises to deal with in a later letter. He has seen St. Paul's Cathedral, but in his opinion the 'large Building here, in which the Head Captain of the Village always dwells', looks more like a rock than does the structure described by 'our great Fore Father, Sa Ga Yean Qua Rash Tow' in the *Spectator.* From a description of the Mansion House the Great Warrior turns to a discussion of the Lord Mayor and Aldermen, explaining that these sachems are not chosen from those distinguished for skill in fighting or oratory, but from those who by trade are 'reckoned worth a great Deal of that shining Ore, which in this Country passes instead of Wampum'.

Thus we see, my dear Brother Yasowa, that it is not the having performed a Number of glorious Actions, but the being possessed of what by them is esteemed more valuable, that gives People a Title to Honours among the English. How different in this Respect are they from the Americans, among whom Merit is the only Passage to Honours, and where a Man is more valued for the Number of Scalps he has taken from the Enemy, than if he were possessed of all the Land that lies between the great River Amazons and the Ohio.

Tohanohawighton then gives his observation on English military government and civil, and commendation of the wine, which once tasted 'thou wouldest never more think of drinking Rum; but, like our Brethren the English, be almost ready to sell even thine own Land for it'.

In any estimate of these literary performances the essayists of the *Universal Spectator* and *St. James's Chronicle* suffer the hazard of writing in a great tradition and submitting to comparison with their masters. The Indian papers by Mr. Bickerstaff and Mr. Spectator remain those that continue to engage the devotee of English prose style in its proper elegance.

Thus did London's Indian visitors of 1710 receive the ceremonial honours, public and private entertainments, and even pictorial perpetuance proper to their heralded station; they appeared in newspaper accounts and periodical comments, diplomatic dispatches, official notations, letters and diaries; and they found their way into such varied publications as epilogue, ballad, occasional poem, prose tract, annal, and essay, composed on demand of purse or self by Anonymous of Grub and Mr. Hack of Fleet Street as well as by Steele and Addison. But as the talk of a talkative Town these Iroquois envoys served as more than a splash of colour: they succeeded in advancing official consideration of the American Indian problem, heartening a martial policy towards Canada, and prodding the Society charged with the cure of foreign souls.

The support England gave her aboriginal auxiliaries was mixed—swift and slow, well planned and ill, benevolent and selfish. For whatever succour she did not send, the four Kings and the Five Nations and all of Indian America had some permanent recompense. In 1712, the year after the large Canadian misadventure, a statue of Anne by Francis Bird was raised in the west front area of St. Paul's Cathedral. Seated around the pedestal on which the Queen stood were four female figures symbolic of Her Majesty's wide power: Britannia holding her trident, Hibernia her harp, Gallia her crown, and America—with head-dress of feathers, a full quiver on her shoulder, and a severed human head under one foot—holding her bow and arrow. The statue of Anne suffered impairment, so that a replica took its place during the reign of Victoria. But Britannia, who briefly lost her trident, remains facing south-west; Hibernia and Gallia are surprisingly unchanged; and the Indian still sits in the churchyard before Wren's greatest monument, which the Kings had visited on their tour of the city and again in the imagination of Addison. Her bow and arrow have been broken.

𝒩otes

FIRST, a note of debt. With characteristic goodwill the following libraries and societies have furnished me information: the British Museum, Public Record Office, Society for the Propagation of the Gospel in Foreign Parts, Royal Society, Bodleian Library, Cambridge University Library, National Library of Scotland, Archives des Affaires Étrangères (Quai d'Orsay), Harvard College Library, Massachusetts Historical Society, Archives Division of the Commonwealth of Massachusetts, American Antiquarian Society, John Carter Brown Library, Yale University Library, New York Public Library, New York Historical Society, Columbia University Library, New York State Library, Library of Congress, Smithsonian Institution, University of Texas Library, Duke University Library, and the Library of the University of North Carolina. I wish to acknowledge the courtesy of the following libraries in granting permission to use the illustrative material appearing in this volume: the New York Public Library, the engraving by Lens and the four engravings by Simon; the Newberry Library, the engraving by Faber; the Trustees of the British Museum, the playbill of Powell's puppet show; and the Lambeth Palace Library, the letter from the sachems to Archbishop Tenison. I am obliged to the Duke of Marlborough for permission to use the Blenheim MSS., to the Earl of Crawford for reproductions of two very scarce items in his great collection, and to Mrs. Robert W. Kelley and Mr. Julian R. Speyers of New York City for permission to use the Vetch Letter Book in their possession.

I am grateful to Yale University for a Sterling fellowship and the University of North Carolina for special grants providing seasons of research during which this pursuit was begun and completed.

My more personal debts are to Marjorie N. Bond, who has shared my stay in King Street; to Professors John Robert Moore of Indiana University and James R. Sutherland of University College, London, for their continued acts of kindness; and to my colleagues, Professors George F. Horner, Hugh T. Lefler, Dougald MacMillan, and Harry K. Russell, who patiently read my manuscript.

NOTES TO CHAPTER I

[In the following notes the place of publication of all books is London unless otherwise stated]

Page 1. THE VISIT. The best, though brief, contemporary account of the visit appeared in Abel Boyer's historical annual, *The History Of the Reign of Queen Anne, Digested into Annals,* ix (1711), 189–91. The most comprehensive later account, not always accurate, is in William Thomas Morgan's article, 'The Five Nations and Queen Anne', *Mississippi Valley Historical Review,* xiii (1926), 169–89.

The proper names of the sachems, quite naturally, suffered various spellings. The series here adopted is that of Boyer's *Annals* and *The Present State of Europe: or, the Historical and Political Monthly Mercury* for April 1710, xxi. 157.

AUDIENCE OF PRESENTATION. Reported in *Dawks's News Letter,* 22 April, the *British Apollo* and *British Mercury,* 21–24 April, and the *Evening Post, Post Boy,* and *Post-Man,* 20–22 April, *Present State of Europe,* xxi. 157, Boyer's *Annals,* ix. 189, and Narcissus Luttrell's *A Brief Historical Relation of State Affairs from September 1678 to April 1714,* Oxford, 1857, vi. 571.

The account of the audience in Dickson's *Dublin Intelligence,* 29 April, adds that the Queen 'promis'd them Her Assistance, and order'd 200 Guineas to be given them' and that they presented her 'with Neck-Laces, Bracelets of Shells, and other Curiosities of their Country, much valuable for the finess of Work'. (Was this Irish paper the source of Swift's first intelligence of the visit?) On the day of the audience the Earl of Sunderland, Secretary of State for the Southern Department, conveyed to the Lord Treasurer the Queen's intention to make a present to the ambassadors from the Five Nations of such things as might be most acceptable to them, and enclosed a list of items to be got ready without loss of time; see Blenheim MSS., Sunderland's Letter Book, ii. 440, and State Papers Domestic, Anne, Public Record Office, S.P. 44/108, p. 226. These gifts are listed above, pp. 12–13.

Pages 1–2. SPEECH TO THE QUEEN. The first printings of the speech, presumably, were two broadsides, differing only in typographical details. One was merely 'Printed in the Year 1710'. The other was printed for and sold by John Baker at the Black Boy in Paternoster Row. The text of the latter is here given from a copy in the collection of the Earl of Crawford, recorded as No. 985 in *Bibliotheca Lindesiana: Catalogue of English Broadsides, 1505–1897,* 1898. This half sheet is entitled *The Four INDIAN KINGS SPEECH To Her MAJESTY*, and the date, 20 April 1710, is followed by the explanation that on the previous day the four princes of the continent of America between New England and Canada had had their public audience *'with great Solemnity'* and made this address.

'GREAT QUEEN!

'WE have undertaken a long and tedious Voyage, which none of our Predecessors could ever be prevail'd upon to undertake. The Motive that induc'd us was, that we might see our *GREAT QUEEN*, and relate to Her those things we thought absolutely necessary for the Good of *HER* and us Her Allies, on the other side the Great Water.

'We doubt not but our *Great Queen*, has been acquainted with our long and tedious War, in Conjunction with Her Children (meaning Subjects) against Her Enemies the French; and that we have been as a strong Wall for their Security, even to the loss of our best Men. The Truth of which our Brother *Queder*, Colonel *Schuyler*, and *Anadagarjaux*, Colonel *Nicholson*, can testify, they having all our Proposals in Writing.

'We were mightily rejoiced when we heard by *Anadagarjaux*, that our Great Queen had resolved to send an Army to reduce *Canada*; from whose Mouth we readily embraced our Great Queen's Instructions; and in Token of our Friendship, we hung up the *Kettle*, and took up the *Hatchet*: and, with one Consent, joined our Brother *Queder*, Colonel *Schuyler*, and *Anadagarjaux*, Colonel *Nicholson*, in making Preparations, on this side the Lake, by building Forts, Store-houses, Canows, and Battows; whilst *Anadiasia*, Colonel *Vetch*, at the same time raised an Army at *Boston*, of which we were informed by our Ambassadors, whom we sent thither for that purpose. We waited long in Expectation of the Fleet from *England*, to join *Anadiasia*, Colonel *Vetch*, to go against *Quebec* by Sea, whilst *Anadagarjaux*, *Queder*, and We, went to *Mont-Royal* by Land; But at last we were told, that our *Great Queen*, by some important Affair, was prevented in Her Design for that Season. This made us extream Sorrowful, lest the *French*, who hitherto had dreaded Us, should now think Us unable to make War against them. The Reduction of *Canada* is of such Weight, that after the effecting thereof, We should have *Free Hunting* and a great Trade with Our *Great Queen*'s Children: and as a Token of the Sincerity of the Six Nations, We do here, in the Name of All, present Our *Great Queen* with these *BELTS* of *WAMPUM*.

'We need not urge to our *Great Queen*, more than the necessity we really labour under obliges us, that in Case our *Great Queen* should not be mindful of us, we must, with our Families, forsake our Country and seek other Habitations, or stand Neuter; either of which will be much against our Inclinations.

'Since we have been in Alliance with our *Great Queen*'s Children, we have had some knowledge of the *Saviour* of the World; and have often been importuned by the *French*, both by the insinuations of their Priests, and by Presents, to come over to their interest, but have always esteem'd them *Men of Falshood*: But if our *Great Queen* will be pleas'd to send over some Persons to instruct us, they shall find a most hearty Welcome.

'We now close all, with Hopes of our *Great Queen*'s Favour, and leave it to Her most Gracious Consideration.'

Early reprintings of the speech appeared in the *Dublin Intelligence*, 29 April 1710, and *Present State of Europe*, xxi. 157–8; the prose tracts *The History and Progress of the four Indian Kings*, 1710, pp. [7–8], and *The Four Kings of Canada*, 1710, pp. 4–6; Boyer's *Annals*, ix. 238–40, and *A Compleat History of Europe* for 1710, pp. 456–7. Later the address appeared in Roger Coke's *A Detection of the Court and State of England*, 4th ed., 1719, iii. 383–4; Daniel Neal's *The History of New-England*, 1720, ii. 602–3; John Oldmixon's *The British Empire in America*, 2nd ed., 1741, i. 247–8; *Westminster Journal: Or, New Weekly Miscellany*, No. 323, 6 February 1748, extracted by the *Gentleman's Magazine*, xviii (1748), 60, and *London Magazine*, xvii (1748), 81; William Smith's *The History of the Province of New-York*, 1757, pp. 122–3; Samuel G. Drake's *Biography and History of the Indians of North America*, Boston, 7th ed., 1837, v. 14–15; 'Extracts from the Manuscripts of Samuel Smith', *Proceedings of the New Jersey Historical Society*, ix (1860), 17; George W. Schuyler's *Colonial New York*, New York, 1885, ii. 34–35; *Calendar of State Papers, Colonial Series, America and West Indies, 1710–June, 1711*, ed. Cecil Headlam, 1924, pp. 78–79: and John Wolfe Lydekker's *The Faithful Mohawks*, Cambridge, 1938, pp. 27–28.

The speech was read to the Queen by Major Pigeon, serving as aide to Schuyler, who was himself as new to England as were the sachems: see *Post Boy* and *Evening Post*, 20–22 April, and Boyer's *Annals*, ix. 189. The Indian's interpreter was Peter Schuyler's cousin, Abraham Schuyler, who petitioned for a reward of his long and many services as interpreter, including those to the four sachems, and was paid £100 for these latter pains and charges: see *Acts of the Privy Council of England, Colonial Series*, A.D. *1680–1720*,

Hereford, 1910, p. 621, and the *Calendar of Treasury Papers, 1708–1714, Preserved in His Majesty's Public Record Office*, ed. Joseph Redington, 1879, p. 176.

The speech gave the *British Apollo*, popular question-and-answer journal, an excuse for not answering a query. The issue of 31 May–2 June 1710, vol. iii, No. 29, contained a question as to 'what Cause brought the Four Kings to our Nation, and how they Succeeded'. Apollo's reply was: 'Their Speech to her Majesty which declares the principal Cause of their coming, being published and so well known might, we thought, have prevented any Application to us upon this Score. But we insert this chiefly to take from hence an occasion to declare, that the Resolution of any Questions concerning Transactions or Consultations of State is foreign to our Design.'

Page 2. 'TWO CROWNS AND CUSHIONS'. Arne's sign is sometimes given as the 'Crown and Cushion' or 'Two Crowns and Cushion', but the double plural has the authority of an advertisement by Arne in the *Post Boy* of 24–27 May 1712, seeking to recover goods taken from the 'Two Crowns and Cushions' at the time of its recent fire. The great damage to 'the House where the *Indian Kings* liv'd' is related in a broadside printed by J. Brown in 1712, *A Full and True Account of a most Cruel and Dreadful Fire*, which describes the house as 'very large and fine' with 'usually several Gentlemen Lodgers'. George H. Cunningham, *London*, 1927, p. 383, locates the birthplace of the younger Thomas Arne as next to the present No. 35, King Street, the original home of the Garrick Club; Hubert Langley, *Doctor Arne*, Cambridge, 1939, p. 12, states that the birthplace of the composer was the site of No. 34, currently occupied by Rivington, the publishing firm.

Arne's lodgings also served the delegation of Cherokees escorted to England from Carolina two decades later by Sir Alexander Cuming, according to a news item in the *St. James's Evening Post* for 30 July–1 August 1730: 'The two Indian Cirakee Kings having taken Leave of their Majesties and the rest of the Royal Family, arrived in Town this Day from Windsor with 5 more Indians of their Attendance, and they have taken Lodgings at Mr. Arne's an Undertaker, in Kingstreet, Covent-Garden, where the four Indian Kings lodged that came over to England in 1710, who we hear recommended their Brethren to the same Lodgings when they set out on their Journey hither.' (See also the *Daily Post* and *Daily Journal*, 3 August.) Thus was Covent Garden revisited twenty years after, without notes on how the Iroquois had got word to the distant Cherokees on a good place to put up while in London.

The King Street of Mohawk lodgement was not, *miserabile dictu*, named in their honour, despite a note to No. 171 in the 1786 edition of the *Tatler* that it was 'a new street which seems at that time to have received the name of King-street'. It had long been so called, and in 1708 had been described under that name by Edward Hatton in his *New View of London*, i. 43.

Pages 2–3. DESCRIPTION OF SACHEMS. *The Four Kings of Canada*, 1710, pp. 6–7. The remainder of the paragraph, pp. 7–8, is as follows: 'According to the Custom of their Country, these Princes do not know what it is to cocker and make much of themselves; nor are they subject to those indispositions our Luxury brings upon us, tho' now among us they live voluptuously. They are not afflicted with Gout, Dropsy, or Gravel; and notwithstanding their Intemperance here, they are not feverish upon any occasion, or troubl'd with Loss of Appetite; for in their own Country they are addicted to Gormandizing, insomuch that they rise in the night to eat; if by good Luck they have meat by them, they fall to it without getting up. It is reported, that these four Princes have been so inur'd to Hunting, and other Sports, that they run as swift as a Deer, and hold it a long Time; so that they propose to run down a Buck or Stag before the Queen, when she pleases to see them, in any of her Parks or Chaces. They are to tire down the Deer, and catch him without Gun, Speare, Launce, or any other Weapon.' The appearance of an advertisement of this tract in the *Post Boy*, 27–29 April, suggests that it was published only ten days after the audience.

The description of the Kings' garments in this pamphlet is apparently the ultimate source of later statements. The best presentation costume for royalty arriving without royal array had posed a problem for the court, still in mourning for the Royal Consort, Prince George of Denmark. In his *History of England, During the Reigns of King William and Queen Mary, Queen Anne, George I*, 1735, p. 452, John Oldmixon explained that the Kings were 'cloath'd by the Playhouse Taylor, like other Kings of the Theatre'.

The native dress of the Kings may have affected the costumes at masquerades. Jeremy Quick in his *Medley: or, Daily Tatler*, No. 8, 29 April 1715, reported going to a masquerade where he 'was interrupted by an *Indian King*, who squees'd my Hand, and very passionately desir'd me to retire into a Private Room'. And an essayist in the *Censor*, No. 28, 5 March 1717, gave his version of what the future historian would say of masquerades: 'Persons of the highest Birth and Stations used frequently to be cloath'd in

Liveries, with *Shoulder-knots:* And those of middle Rank, as their Vanity generally made them aspire, would resemble *Indian Kings,* and *Roman Consuls.*'

Page 3. RICHMOND, GREENWICH, WOOLWICH, AND WHITEHALL. The *Dublin Intelligence,* 2 May, recorded the dinner by the Duke of Ormonde. Boyer's *Annals,* ix. 191, noted their visit to Dr. Flamsteed's in Greenwich Park and their noble treatment by the Admiralty; Luttrell, vi. 572, mentioned the trip by barge, the view of Greenwich Hospital and Woolwich, the entertainment on the yacht, and the visit to Whitehall; the *Post-Man,* 20–22 April, *Dawks's News Letter,* 22 April, and *British Mercury,* 21–24 April, recorded the trip to Greenwich and the yacht.

ILLNESS OF ONE SACHEM. The *Dublin Intelligence,* 6 May, used a London dispatch that one sachem was 'very ill'. Genest (see below, p. 99) concluded his account thus: 'Murphy relates this transaction in his Gray's-Inn Journal, No. 74, but he is not accurate; he supposes it to have taken place at D. L., and speaks of three Indian Kings instead of four.' But Arthur Murphy in his essay on the power of the mob, *Gray's-Inn Journal,* 1756, ii. 271–2, was nearer in time than Genest and correct about the missing King. Sir Justinian Isham confided in his diary that he had seen at the playhouse that day 'three of the W. Indian Kings': H. Isham Longden, 'The Diaries (Home and Domestic) of Justinian Isham, 1704–1736', *Transactions of the Royal Historical Society,* 3rd ser., i (1907), 199. Only three sachems appeared on 25 April before the Council of Trade: see below, p. 100. And Steele's *Tatler* paper of 13 May was grounded on the illness of one of the quartette: see above, p. 80. None of these allusions specifies the ill sachem; the death a few months later of Brant makes him the most likely London sufferer.

Pages 3–5. PERFORMANCES OF PLAYS. The *Daily Courant* repeated its advertisement for *Macbeth* on Saturday and Monday, 22 and 24 April. The performances advertised for the entertainment of the Kings in the *Courant* after *Macbeth* were as follows: for the Haymarket, Tuesday, 25 April, the opera *Almahide* with songs by Nicolini, already praised by Mr. Bickerstaff and to be celebrated by Mr. Spectator; 26 April, Otway's *Venice Preserved*; 27 April, Shadwell's *Squire of Alsatia,* replaced by *Hamlet*; 28 April, Mancini's opera *Hydaspes,* with its lion of later use to Mr. Spectator; Saturday, 29 April, *The Amorous Widow,* with a one-act farce, *The Mayor of Queenborough*; and for Drury Lane on the 25th, *Aurengzebe,* and on the 28th a new comedy called *Squire Brainless*. *The Old Bachelor* and *Macbeth* were also advertised in the *Post Boy*, 18–20 and 20–22 April. Most of these performances and other diversions advertised as for the Kings were noted by Alfred F. Robbins, *Notes & Queries*, 12th ser., ii (1916), 304–5, to which J. S. S., p. 397, added the entry in Genest.

The Haymarket incident is described by John Genest in *Some Account of the English Stage, from the Restoration in 1660 to 1830*, Bath, 1832, ii. 451; he reprinted a portion of the epilogue, pp. 451–2. A copy of this epilogue as a half sheet (from which the lines here are taken) is in the Theatre Collection of the Harvard College Library; it was advertised in the *Supplement*, 21–24 April.

Betterton died 28 April, and Steele gave No. 167 of the *Tatler*, 2–4 May, to an affecting essay on him.

Pages 5–6. COCK-FIGHT, CONCERT, PUPPET-SHOW, AND TRIAL OF SKILL. The advertisement of the cock-fight appeared in the *Daily Courant*, 29 April. A more ecclesiastical cock-match at Cirencester was reported in the *Flying-Post*, 11–13 May, as sponsored by two persons of quality. One cock was called Sacheverell, the other his Dissenter opponent, Burgess. 'It was a very hard Battle, and for a great while Dr. *Sacheverell* had the better, but at last was worsted, and killed by Dr. *Burgesse*, which put an end to the Match, at which some Thousands of Pounds were won and lost.'

The quoted advertisement of the concert appeared in the *Tatler*, No. 165, 27–29 April; similar notices were inserted in the *Daily Courant* for 28 and 29 April. It is to wonder wishfully whether, provided the Kings heard this concert in the Great Room at York Buildings, they were seen there by Richard Steele, who the next year with the musician Thomas Clayton promoted concerts in the Great Room and later created there his Censorium, 'projecting a noble entertainment for persons of a refined taste'.

The handbill for the performance of Powell's puppets, herein reproduced, is in the British Museum, and has been reprinted by John Ashton in *Social Life in the Reign of Queen Anne*, 1882, i. 294.

The advertisement for the trial of skill appeared in the *Daily Courant*, 2 May, and was repeated the next day. For the challenge of a match between Parkes and Hesgate a month earlier see the handbill reprinted from the Bagford Collection by Ashton, *Social Life*, ii. 316. This type of solemn challenge Steele had his own sport with in *Spectator* No. 436, in which Mr. Spectator reports a match at the Bear Garden, Hockley-in-the-Hole, 'a Place of no small

Renown for the Gallantry of the lower Order of *Britons'. Spectator*
No. 449 concludes with a letter from Scabbard Rusty on the friendly
arrangements between two such gladiators for their next quarrel.

Pages 6–7. DUKE OF ORMONDE, COUNCIL OF TRADE, SUN TAVERN,
MERCHANTS, BETHELHEM HOSPITAL, AND WORK-HOUSE. The call on
the Duke was reported in the *Dublin Intelligence*, 2 May.

The visit to the Council of Trade was also reported in the *Dublin
Intelligence*, 2 May, and recorded in the *Journal of the Commissioners
for Trade and Plantations from February 1708–9 to March 1714–5*, 1925,
p. 144.

The *Present State of Europe*, xxi. 158–9, noted the review of the
Guards and printed the speech to the Duke of Ormonde, which
Boyer in his *Annals* of that year, ix. 191, rejected but which was
reprinted in the *Westminster Journal*, No. 323, 6 February 1748, and
in the *Proceedings of the New Jersey Historical Society*, ix (1860), 18,
from the manuscripts of the historian Samuel Smith. The review was
mentioned also in *Dawks's News Letter*, 27 April; in the diplomatic
dispatch of l'Hermitage to the States General, 9 May, B.M. MS.
Add. 17677 DDD, f. 484; in a broadside of 1710, *The Royal Strangers
Ramble*; and by Luttrell, vi. 574. Luttrell in his entry of 20 April, vi.
571, repeated a rumour that the Kings would go over to see the
army in Flanders, but apparently the grenadiers in Hyde Park were
a sufficient military display.

The supper at the Sun Tavern was noted in *Dawks's News Letter*,
27 April.

The entertainment by the merchants was recorded by the *Flying-
Post*, 29 April–2 May, and Luttrell, vi. 576.

The trips to Bethlehem Hospital and the Work-House were reported in *Dawks's News Letter*, 29 April. The *Royal Strangers Ramble*
also mentioned Bedlam.

Pages 7–9. SOCIETY FOR THE PROPAGATION OF THE GOSPEL. The two
standard histories of the early work of the Society (both of which
discuss in some detail the visit of the sachems and its influence)
are by David Humphreys, *An Historical Account of the Incorporated
Society for the Propagation of the Gospel in Foreign Parts*, 1730, and by
its recent archivist, John Wolfe Lydekker, *The Faithful Mohawks*,
Cambridge, 1938. For a wider survey see C. F. Pascoe's *Two Hundred
Years of the S.P.G.*, 2 vols., 1901. However, the full relationship of
the sachems to the Society can be properly followed only in its
archives, including the copies of the Journals and letters. Aspects

of the early history of the Society have been treated by Frank J. Klingberg, 'The Noble Savage as Seen by the Missionary of the Society for the Propagation of the Gospel in Colonial New York 1702–1750', *Historical Magazine of the Protestant Episcopal Church*, viii (1939), 128–65.

For the Queen's instructions see Lydekker, p. 28: for Sunderland's letter to the Archbishop see the S.P.G. 'A' MSS., vol. v, No. 86, and Humphreys, p. 293. For the Archbishop's letter to the secretary of the Society see the 'A' MSS., vol. v, No. 85.

For the Board meeting of 21 April see the S.P.G. Journal, i. 256.

For the meeting of 28 April see the Journal, i. 260–4, quoted passages, pp. 262, 263–4, and 264. The minutes of this meeting are barely summarized in the *Calendar of State Papers, Colonial Series, America and West Indies, 1710–June, 1711*, p. 84. Lydekker reprints, pp. 29–30, the Society's address to the Queen.

For the letter of the sachems, 2 May, see S.P.G. 'A' MSS., vol. v, No. 88, reproduced by Lydekker, pl. iii. For Sunderland's letter to the Treasurer see State Papers Domestic, Anne, Public Record Office, S.P. 44/108, p. 219.

The report of the baptisms appeared in the *Dublin Intelligence*, 9 May.

Page 9. WILLIAM PENN, BISHOP OF LONDON, AND MONTAGUE HOUSE. The dinner with Penn, the sermon and dinner provided by Bishop Compton, and the visit to Montague House were noted in a French dispatch of 2 May, Archives des Affaires Étrangères (Quai d'Orsay), vol. ccxxx, fol. 152.

Few palaces, indeed, could provide more splendour for sight-seeing sachems than Montague House—'composed of fine Brick and Stone Rustick-work, the Roof covered with Slate, and there is an Acroteria of 4 Figures in the Front, being the 4 Cardinal Virtues'; statuary, fountain, gardens, spacious piazza with Ionic columns outside; and inside rich furnishings, finniered floors, noble paintings, and 'the Stair-case and Cupulo-room particularly curious, being Architecture done in Perspective', according to Hatton's *New View of London*, ii. 627–8.

Pages 9–10. UNDATED EVENTS. Leadenhall, Tower, Hockley, Gresham, Exchange, Guildhall, St. Paul's, and Christ's Hospital: the authority for these sights in the Kings' tour is the *Royal Strangers Ramble*. If this broadside poem proceeded accurately and chronologically, the first seven of these places were visited before the royal audience and Christ's Hospital shortly after; however, the *Ramble* also included Bethlehem among the pre-audience points of visit, whereas Dawks (above, p. 100) recorded it as later. Moreover, the Clerk of Christ's Hospital has been able to find no reference to a supper for the Kings in the records of that institution, though, as E. H. Pearce has said in *Annals of Christ's Hospital*, 1901, p. 204: 'It is obvious that a Foundation situated where Christ's Hospital is, wearing a habit such as the Blues still affect, and with the prestige (if nothing more practical) of various Royal patrons, should have an almost prescriptive right to take its part in any ceremonial functions that turn aside the City for a moment from its pursuit of gain.'

The monthly *Present State of Europe*, xxi. 159, referred to 'several Conferences with the Council of Trade'.

The *Evening Post*, 2–4 May, when announcing the departure of the Indians from London, remarked their 'having been magnificently treated by several Persons of Quality during their Stay here'. See also the *Present State*, xxi. 158, and Boyer's *Annals*, ix. 191. The *Dublin Intelligence* on 6 May reported that during the illness of one King 'the other 3 are much carressed and treated by the Nobility, and the other day were nobly entertain'd at the Bishop of Canterburies', and three days later that they 'have been to see most of the Noblemens Houses'.

The allusion to the tradesman's sign appeared in a passage on the *Spectator* essay No. 18, dealing with street signs, in *A Spy upon the Spectator*, Part I, 1711, p. 19.

Page 10. PORTRAITS. For information on the portraits by Lens, Verelst, and Faber see Chapter III of this essay.

Pages 10–11. DANIEL DEMAREE. Boyer's *Annals*, ix. 197–9, 201. For Hearne see his *Remarks and Collections*, ed. C. E. Doble, Oxford, ii (1886), 385. It was the Lady Mayoress who made a 'great Interest to obtain a Reprieve for Demaree' because his wife had nursed several of her Ladyship's children, according to the *Dublin Intelligence*, 9 May, and Carter's *Flying Post* of Dublin, 10 May.

Pages 11–12. PALATINES. The offer of the sachems was believed even by Conrad Weiser, a lad of thirteen when the Indians from 'the promised land of Scorie' went to England. See the entry in his diary, quoted by John Howard Brown, 'The Early German Settlers along the Hudson and Schoharie', *Americana*, viii (1913), 797, and Paul

A. W. Wallace, *Conrad Weiser, 1696–1700, Friend of Colonist and Mohawk*, Philadelphia, 1945, pp. 13–14.

The fact-finding historian who through the Admiralty papers disposed of the legend of Indian beneficence to Aryan is Walter Allen Knittle, *Early Eighteenth Century Palatine Emigration*, Philadelphia, 1937, pp. 150–3.

Daniel Defoe, be it added, opposed sending the Palatines to the colonies but favoured settling them on large forest tracts, 'unimprov'd and unemploy'd', such as that of Sherwood: see his discussions in his comprehensive *Review of the State of the British Nation*, for example, vol. vi, Nos. 43–46, 56–58, 61.

Facts and rumour on the immigrants covered the kingdom and reached America in such an account as the following: 'Almost all sorts of Trades are carrying on in their Camp, which draws daily an incredible Concourse of People from all Parts, out of Curiosity to see this new Palatinate. Where-ever they settle, they will encrease and multiply, for their women are very fruitful, and seldom fail of two at a birth.' This description of the camp, dated 16 August 1709, in London, appeared in No. 308, 6–13 March 1710, of the *Boston News-Letter*, then the only newspaper in the colonies.

Page 12. AUDIENCE OF LEAVE. Recorded by Luttrell, vi. 577. Two versions of a final address to the Queen, together with two versions of a letter to the Privy Council, are printed in the *American Historical Record*, iii (1874), 462–4, from the manuscripts of General Philip Schuyler, now in the New York Public Library.

Page 12. HAMPTON, WINDSOR, AND SOUTHAMPTON. The *Evening Post* and *Post Boy*, 2–4 May, and *Dawks's News Letter*, 4 May, announced the leaving of London for Windsor. The *British Mercury*, 1–3 May, added that the Kings 'were to depart this Morning at three a Clock to Sion-House in the Queen's Barge', and the *Dublin Intelligence*, 9 May, repeated this early hour of setting forth. See also Boyer's *Annals*, ix. 191, and Luttrell, vi. 577.

Word of the visit had carried overland to the north: on 2 May, as the Kings were about to leave London, the jolly vicar of Barwick, George Plaxton, wrote to his friend and neighbour at Leeds, the learned Ralph Thoresby:

'What is become of old Sydrophil? I cannot tell whether he be upon earth or gone to his beloved starrs; none can tell me, 'tis a secret in his own keeping. I have heard nothing from him since passive obedience was baited, and the Homilies try'd for their lives before the Bᵖˢ. I fancy my old friend the Mysta of Leeds has made a trip to London to visit the 4 Indian monarchs and to get an autograph of his Majesty King Anadagarjaux, though if I had been to advise him he should have asked a belt of wampum from good King Quedor; I am told that the Corporation of L. is sending an envoy to them to perswade 'em to weare clothes and bring coats and breeches in fashion among their subjects; this will mend trade and help of[f] the woollen manufacture, but the grandees of York I feare will get the start and recommend their thinn stuffs for summer matchcoats if a speedy application be not made to those potent hero's. If the town of L. send up an envoy, I hope a frᵈ of mine will be the man. Well, Ralpho, where-ever thou art, alive or dead, on earth or in the ayr, if this finds thee let it give you my hearty service. I have the same affection for you in all places and in all conditions; nothing can alter the friendᵖ, affections, services, duties, love, respects, and good wishes of

My dear Fauste,
Yours very truly,
Barwick.

'My service to the Recorder; who knows but he may be a Lᵈ Cheif Justice of Quebeck, and John Killingbeck Primate of Orenoque, if these Indians be baptized and come into the Union with Engl. and Scotland. Pray del[iver] to the Recorder.'

Letters Addressed to Ralph Thoresby, ed. W. T. Lancaster (Publications of the Thoresby Society, xxi), Leeds, 1912, pp. 213–14. The Recorder of Leeds was Richard Thornton, and Killingbeck the Vicar.

Pages 12–13. GIFTS. The invoice of merchandise bought for the sachems is noted in the *Calendar of Treasury Papers, 1708–1714*, p. 178; this Public Record Office document is T.1/121, No 52, dated 29 April 1710, and signed by James Douglas, for whom see above, p. 43.

The purification lath and two tump-lines are recorded as items 572, 573, and 574 in the manuscript catalogue of Miscellanies in Sloane's Collection, and may be seen in the Department of Ethnography of the British Museum; the prisoners' ropes recorded in another entry (No. 1535) are not available. There is a reference to these prisoners' cords in the notes to No. 171 of the 1786 *Tatler*.

Page 13. DEPARTURE. The dates in the shipping news show some disagreement; those adopted here represent the consensus.

Arrived at Spithead the 6th: *Post-Man*, 6–9 May, *British Mercury*, 8–10 May, *British Apollo*, 7–9 May.

On *Royal Sovereign* the 7th: *Evening Post*, 9–11 May, *Post-Man*, 9–11 May, *Supplement*, 8–10 May.

Sailed from Spithead the 8th: *Flying-Post*, 9–11 May, *London Gazette*, 9–11 May, *Post-Man*, 9–11 May, *Supplement*, 8–10 May.

Arrived at Plymouth the 10th: *Daily Courant*, 16 May, *London Gazette*, 13–16 May, *Post Boy*, 13–16 May, *Post-Man*, 13–16 May, *British Mercury*, 15–17 May.

Sailed from Plymouth and returned the 14th: *Daily Courant*, 20 May, *Evening Post*, 18–20 May, *Post Boy*, 16–18 May and 18–20.

Sailed from Plymouth the 19th: *Daily Courant*, 23 May, *Evening Post*, 20–23 May, *London Gazette*, 20–23 May.

The entertainment by the Admiral was recorded in the *Post-Man*, 9–11 May. Some portion of Lord Aylmer's fame is associated with the Kings: the legend on one of his portraits reads 'who entertained the Four Kings on board the Royal Sovereign, 1710'. See R. H. S. in *Notes and Queries*, 2nd ser., viii (1859), 417.

For the apparition see *The Age of Wonders* [1710, p. 1].

Pages 14–15. LETTERS FROM NICHOLSON, SACHEMS, AND SCHUYLERS. The four letters by Nicholson of 12, 14 (twice), and 22 May are quoted in the *Calendar of State Papers, Colonial Series, America and West Indies 1710–June, 1711*, pp. 98, 103, 103–4, and 105.

Nicholson's letter to the Archbishop, dated 22 May, is MS. 941.24 in the Lambeth Palace Library; for a copy see S. P. G. 'A' MSS., vol. v, No. 94. Copies of the letters by the sachems and by Schuyler to the Archbishop are 'A' MSS., vol. v, Nos. 93 and 95.

For the letters, also dated 22 May, to Sunderland from the sachems (signed with their totem marks) and the Schuylers see Henry E. Huntington Library MSS. 348 and 22270.

Page 15. ARRIVAL IN BOSTON. Boyer's *Annals*, ix (1711), 191. See also below, p. 122.

Pages 15–16. 'HAVING SEEN OUR STATE' AND 'MEN OF GOOD PRESENCE'. The lines by Cowper are from the passage on Omai, the Society Islander brought to England in 1774: *The Task*, 1785, i. 642–5.

The favourable estimate of the sachems appeared in the *Present State of Europe*, April 1710, xxi. 160.

Page 16. OTHER VISITS. Although this visit of 1710 constitutes the first official embassy of American sachems, Indians had, of course, been seen in London long before the time of Anne. For example, two of Raleigh's captains took home with them the good Manteo, 'Lord of Roanoke', and the not good Wanchese. Squanto of New England was taken to England. And Mrs. John Rolfe of Virginia (daughter of Powhatan, who was himself subjected to coronation as Emperor by the English) pleased the King and Queen and courtiers, was entertained by the Lord Bishop of London with 'Festivall state and pompe', and died at Gravesend in 1616. But such early visits, howsoever useful or pleasant, carried small resemblance to the prototype established by the journey of the Mohawk envoys in 1710.

The next visit by Indians, in 1719–20, drew no large notice. In Mist's *Weekly Journal*, 22 August, 1719, there appeared the following notice: 'Last Week three Indian Kings appeared in this City; they seemed to be of some extraordinary Savage Extraction, and carried themselves with extraordinary Reservedness, and a Majestick Deportment; All Things they did and said having something of the King in them: but on a sudden they have disappeared, and some will have it be, that they walk'd off in the Night without Shoes or Stockings; but we are loath to detract from the Royal Dignity so much, tho' it be in the Persons of Foreigners, as to think they should run away bare-footed.' Defoe commented on these reputed princes, now two in number, in the *Weekly Journal*, 2 January 1720, and their poor treatment 'for the Entertainment of the Rabble' got strong protest in No. 32, 18 April, of the *Commentator*, a journal attributed to Defoe by John Robert Moore. See also *Applebee's Original Weekly Journal*, 26 March, and a letter from the comedian James Spiller in Steele's *Anti-Theatre*, No. 13, 29 March, and the reply in No. 15, 4 April.

The first important visit after that of the New Yorkers was made by Cherokee chiefs, escorted in 1730 by Sir Alexander Cuming to resign their Crown of Tennessee to their white German father, George II: see also above, p. 96, and Verner W. Crane, *The Southern Frontier, 1670–1732*, Durham, N.C., 1928, pp. 279–80, 295–302. Four years later Oglethorpe (who might as a boy have seen the Mohawk sachems in London) brought Tomochichi, his family, and four other Creek chieftains: see Charles C. Jones, jr., *Historical Sketch of Tomo-chi-chi, Mico of the Yamacraws*, Albany, 1868, pp. 58–76, and Amos Aschbach Ettinger, *James Edward Oglethorpe, Imperial Idealist*, Oxford, 1936, pp. 144–7. In 1762 Henry Timberlake escorted the King of the Cherokees and two chiefs to England, where 'their Cherokeeships' were received with great splendour, much comment, and some criticism. In the sixties there were other Indian visits of a minor character and the long stay of Samson Occom, the Mahican missionary. And in 1776 Joseph Brant, grandson to the King of the Maquas, made a famous triumphal trip, sat to Romney for his portrait and the July *London Magazine* for a sketch, and was entertained by James Boswell, expert in celebrity. For historical and literary surveys see Carolyn Thomas Foreman, *Indians Abroad, 1493–1938*, Norman, Okla., 1943, and Benjamin Bissell, *The American Indian in English Literature of the Eighteenth Century*, New Haven, 1925.

A review of visits may well be concluded with a minor but interesting incident of 1765, of which the facts can be assembled from the *Letters and Papers of Cadwallader Colden, 1765–1775, Collections of the New-York Historical Society*, lvi (1923), 23, 38–39, 41; *Parliamentary History of England, 1765–1771*, xvi (1813), 50–52; *Journal of the Commissioners for Trade and Plantations . . . 1764–1767*, pp. 155–6, 157–9, 161; and Public Record Office, C.O. 388/84, P. 185, P. 189. In short, a complaint was made to the House of Lords that two Mohawks, named Hermannus and Joseph, had been brought from New York by a Jew named Hyam Myers and exhibited to public view at an ale-house in London. Their Lordships, averse to exploitation, 'thought proper to interpose their Authority to prevent so scandalous a Proceeding'. Joseph and Hermannus were accordingly sent home with a responsible person to conduct them at the expense of the Government, the account of costs totalling £108 and including passage, provisions, bedding, clothes, guns, coloured prints of the King and Queen, and pinchbeck medals of His Majesty the third George. Thus did a foster nation bring wisdom and grace to the care of two of its misplaced Mohawks, who were not Kings—six years after a coalition of Anglo-American-Indian arms had gained Montreal and Quebec in the final Glorious Enterprise, which brought Canada to England.

NOTES TO CHAPTER II

Pages 17–19. BACKGROUND. The most detailed book on the Indian background is *The Bloody Mohawk*, by T. Wood Clarke, New York, 1940. The most authoritative survey of the New York background may be found in the first two volumes, *Wigwam and Bouverie* and *Under Duke and King*, of the ten-volume symposium, *History of the State of New York*, edited by Alexander C. Flick and published under the auspices of the New York State Historical Association, New York, 1933; the chapter by Arthur H. Buffinton, 'The Colonial Wars and Their Results', ii. 203–46, is an especially clear and perceptive account.

Pages 19–22. SCHUYLER, NICHOLSON, AND VETCH. Accounts of these three figures all appear in the volumes of the *Dictionary of American Biography*, and the latter two as well in the *Dictionary of National Biography*. The only echoes of discord among these leaders are unverified and distant reports in easily prejudiced French letters: see *Documents Relative to the Colonial History of the State of New-York*, procured by John Romeyn Brodhead, ed. E. B. O'Callaghan, ix (1885), 839, 843. [Hereinafter the title of this work will be abbreviated to *Docs. Rel. N.Y.*]

The most detailed biographical account of Schuyler is in George W. Schuyler's *Colonial New York: Philip Schuyler and His Family*, 2 vols., New York, 1885: see ii. 37, for the Queen's gifts and offer of a knighthood. The full-length portrait of Schuyler, wearing a sword and red costume, was in 1923 presented to the City of Albany and hangs in the office of the Mayor. This unsigned picture has been attributed to Kneller but is not included in the chronological catalogue of some of Kneller's principal works in Lord Killanin's *Sir Godfrey Kneller and His Times, 1646–1723*, 1948, pp. 97–100. It is reproduced in Clarke's *Bloody Mohawk*, p. 103, and the *History of the State of New York*, ed. Flick, ii. 214. The vase given Schuyler by the Queen was thus inscribed: 'Presented by Anne Queen of England to Col. Peter Schuyler, of Albany, in the Province of New York, April 19, 1710. To commemorate his visit to England by request of the Provincial government, accompanied by five sachems of the Mohawks.' See James Grant Wilson, *Annual Report of the American Historical Association for the Year 1891*, 1892, p. 297, n., repeated, with a picture of the vase, in *The Memorial History of the City of New-York*, New York, ii (1892), 117, n. 2, and *National Magazine*, xvii (1893), 212, n. 3. Anne Grant, *Memoirs of an American Lady*, 1808, i. 26–27, furnished reasons for Schuyler's declining the knighthood: 'being pressed to assign his reasons, he said he had brothers and near relations in humble circumstances, who, already his inferiors in property, would seem as it were depressed by his elevation: and though it should have no such effect on her mind, it might be the means of awakening pride or vanity in the female part of his family.' Anne Grant elaborated the stay in England of Schuyler (whom she rechristens Philip) as he consorted with the great men of that day (including Marlborough, who was not then in England), and returned home with the great literary works of that era (including some not then published).

Pages 22–24. PROPOSAL FOR EXPEDITION. For Vetch's 'Canada Survey'd' see the *Calendar of State Papers, Colonial Series, America and West Indies, June, 1708–1709, Preserved in the Public Record Office,* ed. Cecil Headlam, 1922, pp. 41–51, quoted passages, pp. 41, 51. [The title of a volume in this truly monumental set will hereinafter be abbreviated to *C.S.P., Amer.,* with the inclusive dates of the pertinent volume.] For Vetch's supplements see pp. 147–50 and 163–4. For the deliberations of the Council of Trade see pp. 57–58, 61, 89, 163–4, 164–5, 177, and the *Journal of the Commissioners for Trade and Plantations, 1704–9,* pp. 530–2, 534–5, 547, 553–7, 559. Vetch's per diem pay is recorded in the *Calendar of Treasury Papers, 1708–14,* p. 55. His letter to Sunderland, 15 June, is in the Blenheim MSS. C.I. 41. For a letter from Vetch to Sunderland of 10 August begging to know whether he should stay in England to assist with the scheme or sail home the next week with Lord Lovelace see State Papers Domestic, Anne, Public Record Office, S.P. 34/10, No. 11.

In 1696 John Nelson, a man of affairs in New England with knowledge of Canada, suggested to the Council of Trade a scheme for the reduction of the French: *C.S.P., Amer., 1696–97,* pp. 138–40. His proposal was that of a concurrent descent on Montreal and Quebec, with some of the same details Vetch was to include. Nelson clearly saw that 'What will especially facilitate the enterprise will be that wherever our forces first attack, it will call their whole strength from one end of the river to the other, so that either one or the other will be left naked', p. 140. He had earlier presented the idea to Shrewsbury, the then Secretary of State for the Southern Department: Historical Manuscripts Commission, *Report on the Manuscripts of the Duke of Buccleuch & Queensberry,* ii (1903), 729–33. For Nelson's suggestion to send Indians to England see below, p. 113. Six years later Lord Cornbury, Governor of New York, in some detail proposed to the Council of Trade a joint attack on Quebec and Montreal, 'a very feazable thing': *C.S.P., Amer., 1702,* pp. 628–9. On a visit to New York the next April Colonel Nicholson, then Governor of Virginia, agreed with Cornbury about the proposal and asked the Lords of Trade that he be second in command of such an expedition or at least go with the New York Governor as a volunteer: *C.S.P., Amer., 1702–3,* pp. 567–8. Cornbury wrote the Council of Trade as late as 1708 that he was of the same opinion still on the advantage and facility of forcing the French from Canada. This letter was received after the Council had made its representation to the Secretary of State on Vetch's proposal of a like nature, so that only an extract was enclosed to Sunderland to lay before the Queen: *C.S.P., Amer., 1708–9,* pp. 71, 177. Governor Dudley was, of course, close to Vetch and much interested in the reduction of Canada, and promoted attempts on Port Royal: see Chapter VI in Everett Kimball's *The Public Life of Joseph Dudley,* New York, 1911, and *C.S.P., Amer., 1706–8,* pp. 31, 148, 240, 591.

Thomas Hutchinson, *The History of the Colony and Province of Massachusetts-Bay,* ed. Lawrence Shaw Mayo, Cambridge, Mass., 1936, ii. 123, considered it well known that in 1707 an armament from England under General George MacCartney was intended against the French, 'but the battle of Almanza, in Spain, made such an alteration in affairs, that the troops could not be spared, and the expedition was laid aside'.

Pages 24–25. INSTRUCTIONS IN 1709. For the Queen's instructions to Vetch see *C.S.P., Amer., 1708–9,* pp. 230–2, and for her letter to Lovelace, pp. 232–3. The instructions have been reprinted in the *Collections of the Nova Scotia Historical Society for the Year 1884,* iv. 64–68, and the *Pennsylvania Magazine of History and Biography,* xxxviii (1914), 340–4. For the appointment of Vetch as Adjutant-General see State Papers Domestic, Anne, Public Record Office, S.P. 44/178, p. 77.

For Sunderland's letter of 28 April to Lovelace (who died prior to receipt) see *C.S.P., Amer., 1708–9,* pp. 283–5; his letter to Dudley, pp. 285–6; and his like letters to Rhode Island, Connecticut, and Pennsylvania, p. 286.

For the instructions to Brigadier Thomas Whetham, commander of the troops, dated 20 April, see Public Record Office, C.O. 5/9, No. 24; for his additional instructions of 7 and 9 May, *C.S.P., Amer., 1708–9,* pp. 295, 297. His commission was signed 9 May according to an account of the intended expedition based on Sunderland's papers, B.M. MS. Add. 32694, f. 110. Thomas Erle had been considered for this command: State Papers Domestic, Anne, S.P. 34/10, No. 96. Rear-Admiral John Baker was to command the fleet. For deliberations on the preparation of the expedition see the minutes of the Committee of Council, 20, 30 December 1708, and 3 January, 21, 26 February, 1709, Blenheim MSS. C. I. 16. In these archives is also a careful memorandum on the preparations.

The especially interesting letter to Sunderland from Vetch and Nicholson in Portsmouth, 11 March 1709, is in the Blenheim MSS. C.I. 41. Among the same papers is a proposal for an earlier American conquest in the reverse order, endorsed by one Clements 6 June 1708; with the depletion of the French the English might reimburse themselves for the expenses of the war by reducing the West Indies and then attempting Newfoundland and Canada.

There may have been some intention for the expedition to proceed to Newfoundland if its conquest of Quebec had been finished by the end of August, or if the season had been too advanced to consider some other service: see C.O. 5/9, No. 24.

Pages 25–26. VETCH AND NICHOLSON TO SUNDERLAND, 28 JUNE. *C.S.P.*, *Amer.*, *1708–9*, pp. 399–406, quoted passage, p. 405. For Vetch's letters to Boyle and Sunderland see pp. 398–9. For the difficulties in Jersey and Pennsylvania see also pp. 349, 406, 409–10, 411–15. For Nicholson's letter to Sunderland see pp. 419–20.

The reference by Mather appears in his diary under 3 May 1709, *Massachusetts Historical Society Collections*, 7th ser., viii (1912), 8.

The New York commissions of Nicholson as Commander-in-Chief of all the forces against Canada and of Schuyler as Commander of the Indian forces are entered in the *Calendar of New York Colonial Commissions*, *1680–1770*, abstracted by Edmund B. O'Callaghan, New York, 1929, p. 15. Vetch and Nicholson had on 17 May communicated the Queen's instructions to the Council and Assembly of New York: *Journal of the Legislative Council Of the Colony of New-York . . . 1691–1743*, Albany, 1861, i. 278–9.

Page 27. RESOLUTION OF NEW YORK COUNCIL. Council Minutes, 21 June 1709, x. 679–80, abstracted in *Calendar of Council Minutes*, *1668–1783*, New York State Library, Bulletin 58, History 6, Albany, 1902, p. 229.

Pages 27–28. VETCH TO SUNDERLAND, 2 AND 12 AUGUST. *C.S.P.*, *Amer.*, *1708–9*, pp. 437–9, quoted passage, p. 437.

For the proclamation by Governor Dudley of the Fast on 15 September see *C.S.P.*, *Amer.*, *1710–11*, p. 30.

Page 28. GILES DYER AND JUDGE SEWALL. For the bill for the dinner by order of Dyer see Massachusetts Archives, xxxi. 76.

For the record in Sewall's diary see *Sewall Papers*, vol. ii, *Collections of the Massachusetts Historical Society*, 5th ser., vi (1879), 261.

Justin Winsor confuses this visit to Boston with that to England in his *Narrative and Critical History of America*, Boston and New York, v (1887), 107. In their address to Anne (above, p. 94) the Kings mentioned their sending ambassadors to Boston.

Pages 29–30. VETCH TO NICHOLSON, 12 AUGUST AND 12 SEPTEMBER. Letter of 12 August, Vetch Letter Book, pp. 60–61, quoted passage, p. 60; letter of 12 September, pp. 62–63, quoted passages, p. 62. This letter book, now in the possession of descendants of Colonel Vetch, Mrs. Robert W. Kelley and Mr. Julian R. Speyers of New York, is a most excellent mirror of the proceedings of 1709–10 because Vetch, at the centre of things, kept such a full record of the correspondence, most of which has not been published. These new letters, added to other fresh material, make possible now a close account of the situation which preceded and produced the visit of the sachems.

Governor Dudley on 31 January 1710 wrote to the Council of Trade and enclosed the 'Account of charges accruing to the Massachusetts Bay, from the intended expedition to Canada', which included an item of £109 'To charge upon 6 Maquas that came down to see the fleet': *C.S.P., Amer., 1710–11*, p. 30. This letter travelled on the ship that took the four sachems to England, and was read in Council the day after they were received by the Queen.

Page 31. VETCH TO SUNDERLAND, 12 SEPTEMBER. Vetch Letter Book, pp. 66–67, quoted passages, p. 66; postscript, pp. 67–68. This letter has been published in a privately printed pamphlet by J. Clarence Webster, *Samuel Vetch*, 1929, pp. 19–21.

For the letters from the Assembly at Newport, Rhode Island, 3 September, and from Governor Dudley of Massachusetts, 8 September, desiring a decrease in the forces from those colonies, see Vetch Letter Book, pp. 63–64 and 64.

Pages 31–32. VETCH TO GOVERNORS, 13 SEPTEMBER. Vetch Letter Book, pp. 64–65, quoted passage, p. 65.

Pages 32–33 OFFICERS TO VETCH, 2 SEPTEMBER. Vetch Letter Book, pp. 70–71, quoted passage, p. 70. This important letter, like the action of the New York Council, has apparently not hitherto been used in any discussion of the embassy of the four sachems.

Page 33. ORIGIN OF PROPOSAL. Among the historians who have fathered Schuyler with the project of conducting (five) chieftains are William Smith, *History of the Province of New-York*, p. 121; William Dunlap, *History of the New Netherlands, Province of New York, and State of New York*, New York, i (1839), 269; William L. Stone, *The Life and Times of Sir William Johnson, Bart.*, Albany, 1865, i. 26; James Grant Wilson, *Memorial History of the City of New York*, ii. 119. Dunlap and Wilson state that the trip was at Schuyler's expense, and Dunlap adds that Schuyler wished to persuade the Queen and her husband (who had died in October of 1708).

George W. Schuyler, *Colonial New York*, p. 32, says that Nicholson and Schuyler resolved on the trip and took the chiefs in imitation of the French. For the French precedent see, for example, *Doc. Rel. N.Y.*, ix. 437, 439, 464, 544. It is particularly interesting here to observe that a French proposal of 1731 to send chiefs to see their King used as argument the English precedent: ibid. ix. 1030–1.

John Nelson noted that six sagamores at the time of his writing in 1696 were at Versailles to solicit help against the English. He predicted that sending chiefs to England would 'give counterpoise to the French reputation and greatness, which a sight of the City of London and of what else may be shewed them here, or if need be in Flanders, will easily effect. For those whom we have brought over, being unable to conceive anything greater than we have shewn them, will return home, and by their report of our numbers, strength, riches, etc., will encourage our friends and regain for us the waverers, so that we shall equal our reputation to that of the French.' 'Memorial of John Nelson to Council of Trade', *C.S.P., Amer., 1696–97*, p. 135. Nelson earlier had written likewise to Shrewsbury: Historical Manuscripts Commission, *Report on the Manuscripts of the Duke of Buccleuch & Queensberry*, ii (1903), 726.

As to previous efforts to send chiefs to England, Vetch wrote Pringle, 10 February 1710, 'Nothing but Coll Schuylers coming along would have prevailed with them to have undertaken such a voyage, which my Ld Bellamont and all the Governours of New York hath endeavoured to persuade them to before, so you may safely believe they are in earnest': J. Clarence Webster, *Samuel Vetch*, p. 21. See also the letter by Vetch and Dudley to Sunderland, 9 January 1710, p. 42 above; the letter from Vetch to Sunderland, 1 February 1710, Vetch Letter Book, p. 114; and his letter to Godolphin, n.d., ibid., p. 117. In their address to the Queen the sachems had themselves said that none of their predecessors had ever been prevailed upon to undertake the voyage: see above, p. 94.

Pages 33–35. NEWS OF PACQUET. See letters by Vetch, 3 October, to Ingoldsby, Nicholson, and Saltonstall in Vetch Letter Book, pp. 76, 77, and 77, all mentioning the express from court and proposing to delay the Congress. The news from Wood Creek was relayed from Saltonstall to Vetch in a letter of 6 October: ibid., pp. 78–79. A letter from Ingoldsby to Vetch, 26 September, had expressed the view of New York: ibid., p. 74.

On 11 October Vetch and Nicholson at Newport wrote to Dudley desiring his presence, to the officers at Wood Creek concerning the fort, and to Ingoldsby: ibid., pp. 80–81, 81–82, and 82–83. On the same day Dudley wrote from Roxbury to Vetch that the pacquet had arrived: ibid., p. 83.

The interval of some four months between the decision to give over the expedition and its receipt in America accumulated from delays in the sailing and the voyage of the pacquet (as the colonists knew) and in a lack of promptness in setting the message on its way (as the colonists could not well know). As early as 30 May Sunderland had directed Whetham to come to receive Her Majesty's further commands, she judging it fit to make some alterations in his orders: State Papers Domestic, Anne, Public Record Office, S.P. 44/108, p. 97^v, and Blenheim MSS., Sunderland Letter Book, ii. 290. On 5 June Godolphin wrote Marlborough that on that day the decision had been made to send Admiral Baker's squadron and seven regiments to join in an attempt against Granada, Andalusia, and Cadiz: B.M. MS. Add. 9105, f. 81. On 11 June the Cabinet Council decided that General Whetham should discharge his expedition and an advice boat carry the word to New England that the ships and troops intended for the expedition would be better employed elsewhere and that the forces got together in America should make some attempt on Nova Scotia: Blenheim MSS., C.I.16. The same day Sunderland informed Whetham that the Queen had put to one side for some time the designed expedition: B.M. MS. Add. 32694, f. 110^v, S.P. 44/108, p. 91, and Sunderland Letter Book, ii. 295. On 24 June Sunderland wrote the Lord High Admiral that there was an occasion for a dispatch boat to New York: Public Record Office, Adm. 1/4093, No. 78. On 1 July he wrote the bad news to America: Vetch Letter Book, p. 84; *C.S.P., Amer., 1708–9*, p. 408; and Adm. 1/4083, No. 84.

Pages 33–35. CONGRESS OF GOVERNORS. For the proceedings of the Congress and the address to the Queen see *C.S.P., Amer., 1708–9*, pp. 490–2, quoted passages, p. 490. For the somewhat similar letter to the Queen signed by sixty-seven citizens see pp. 492–3.

Godolphin considered that the sixteenth article in the Peace preliminaries, which stipulated mutual restitution by England and France of all places in America taken from each other during the war, made fruitless an expedition thither. This development in the Peace negotiations provided a reason for diverting the ships from America, a reason which coincided with a desire to use them at the Peninsula. See Godolphin's letters to Marlborough, 31 May 1709, B.M. MS. Add. 9105, f. 63ᵛ, and 20 April 1710, MS. Add. 9108, f. 172ᵛ.

Pages 35–36. LETTERS TO SHIP CAPTAINS. Letter to Captain George Martin, 19 October, *C.S.P.*, *Amer.*, *1708–9*, p. 495; letters to Captains Mathews, Smith, Clifton, and Davis of same date, pp. 494–5.

In a letter to Sunderland of 24 October, in which they stated their case and enclosed the resolutions of the Congress and its address to the Queen, Vetch, Nicholson, Dudley, and Moody recounted the refusal of the ship captains and, to prevent some later confusion of divided authority, recommended a single command for the next expedition: ibid., pp. 488–9.

Page 36. DEPARTURE OF NICHOLSON. For the imminent sailing of Nicholson, the hope of others to follow, and the needs of the spring offensive see the letter to Sunderland from Vetch, Dudley, and Moody, 25 October, ibid., p. 497. On the same day Vetch wrote Sunderland's secretary asking for the chief command and suggesting Nicholson for the government of New York: Webster, *Samuel Vetch*, pp. 8–9.

A letter from Vetch and Nicholson on 28 October to Colonel Redknap stated that Nicholson and Moody planned to go aboard the *Dragon* that day: Vetch Letter Book, p. 98. On the 31st Vetch wrote Ingoldsby that they had sailed, pp. 100–1. Nicholson was in London by 6 December: see Public Record Office, C.O. 5/9, Nos. 32, 33. James Grant Wilson, 'An Acadian Governor', *International Review*, xi (1881), 481, n., asserts that Nicholson was accompanied by several gentlemen and representatives from each of the Five Nations; Francis Parkman, *A Half-Century of Conflict*, 1892, i. 141, notes the sailing of Nicholson in December; and Lydekker, *Faithful Mohawks*, p. 25, says that both Vetch and Nicholson sailed for England in December.

The Deputy Governor, Council, and Representatives of Connecticut requested and appointed Governor Saltonstall to attend Her

Majesty and manage the affairs of their government mentioned in the address agreed upon by the Congress of Governors, and granted him £200 for the charge of his agency and as a recompense. Saltonstall did not go. See *The Public Records of the Colony of Connecticut . . . 1706–1716*, ed. Charles J. Hoadly, Hartford, 1870, pp. 139–40.

Page 37. VETCH TO SUNDERLAND, LORD TREASURER, AND OTHERS. Vetch to the Secretary of State, 24 October, Vetch Letter Book, pp. 94–95; to Lord Godolphin and Lord Somers, 25 October, pp. 96–97 and 97. Letter to Queensberry, 16 November, ibid., pp. 104–5; to Lord Stair, Sunderland, the Lord Treasurer, and the Duke of Argyle, 18 November, pp. 105–6, 106, 107, and 108: to Mr. Pringle and Mr. Mason (for influence with the Earl of Orkney and the Duke of Hamilton), 18 November, pp. 109 and 109–10.

Page 38. SELECTION OF KINGS. Concerning the status and prestige of the chosen four sachems see above, p. 58, for Barclay's dissent in a letter of 26 September 1710 to the S.P.G. Hunter in 1713 wrote to the home government, 'Happily indeed for us those who were carryed to England were men of no consideration or rather the most obscure amongst them', though conceding Hendrick 'some credit with the small village of Mohaks called Scoharee': *C.S.P., Amer., 1712–14*, pp. 158–9. In 1727 a French document commented as follows: 'That was a pure farce that was acted in England, where these pretended Ambassadors were carried around as Iroquois Princes and Indian Kings, who were come to lay at the Queen's feet their Crowns, as people called a paltry ornament common to all Indians, and which among them is a token neither of honour nor of dignity. These pretended Ambassadors were nothing more than *Parkailers* of no character: neither Chiefs nor deputies from the Chiefs or Council of the Nation, who in their hearts ridiculed the grand part they were made to perform, and have since been disavowed by the Five Nations, who delegated to them neither power, commission, nor character': *Doc. Rel. N.Y.*, ix. 983. And Cadwallader Colden, in a passage derogatory of Peter Schuyler, referred to his 'carrying to England five or six common Indians': *Letters on Smith's History of New York, Collections of the New-York Historical Society for the Year 1868*, 1868, p. 200.

In *A Compleat History of Europe* for 1710, p. 458, a statement that one of the Kings 'spoke *High Dutch*, and some said his Father was a Native of *Germany*' may mean only that one sachem had caught a number of Dutch phrases from the traders at Albany.

Boston had in 1710 about 9,000 inhabitants, New York less than 6,000: Carl Bridenbaugh, *Cities in the Wilderness*, New York, 1938, p. 143, n.

Page 39. NUMBER OF KINGS. Among the historians, old and new, who have been content with four Kings are Daniel Neal, *History of New-England*, ii. 602; David Humphreys, *Historical Account*, p. 292; Paul Chamberlen, *An Impartial History of the Life and Reign Of . . . Queen Anne*, 1738, p. 347; William Maitland, *The History of London, from its Foundation by the Romans, to the Present Time*, 1739, p. 325; Samuel Smith, *The History of the Colony of Nova-Caesaria, or New-Jersey*, Burlington, New Jersey, 1765, p. 366; Justin Winsor, *Narrative and Critical History of America*, v. 107; John Fiske, *The Dutch and Quaker Colonies in America*, 1899, ii. 242; Arthur H. Buffington, *History of the State of New York*, ii. 221; George Macaulay Trevelyan, *The Peace and the Protestant Succession* (*England Under Queen Anne*, vol. iii), 1934, p. 142. The *American Historical Record*, iii. 463, records that one of the four died in England.

Members of the five-King school include William Smith, *History Of the Province of New-York*, p. 121; Peter Kalm, *Travels Into North America*, trans. John Reinhold Foster, Warrington, 1770, London, 1771, i. 268; Samuel G. Drake, *Biography and History of the Indians of North America*, v. 13; Richard Hildreth, *The History of the United States of America*, New York, 1856, ii. 261; Charles De Wolf Brownell, *The Indian Races of North and South America*, New York, 1858, p. 326; John McMullen, *The History of Canada, from its First Discovery to the Present Time*, Brockville, 2nd ed., 1868, p. 89; E. M. Ruttenber, *History of the Indian Tribes of Hudson's River*, Albany, 1872, p. 188, n. 3; John Hill Burton, *A History of the Reign of Queen Anne*, Edinburgh and London, 1880, iii. 88; Francis Parkman, *A Half-Century of Conflict*, 1892, i. 141; Sanford H. Cobb, *The Story of the Palatines*, New York and London, 1897, p. 104; Francis Whiting Halsey, *The Old New York Frontier*, New York, 1901, p. 158; William Thomas Morgan, *Mississippi Valley Historical Review*, xiii. 178; Walter Allen Knittle, *Early Eighteenth Century Palatine Emigration*, p. 150; John Wolfe Lydekker, *Faithful Mohawks*, p. 25; T. Wood Clarke, *Bloody Mohawk*, p. 113; Carolyn Thomas Foreman, *Indians Abroad*, p. 34; and R. W. G. Vail, 'The Portraits of "The Four Kings of Canada", a Bibliographical Footnote', *To Doctor R.*, Philadelphia, 1946, p. 218. Of these Drake, Parkman, Cobb, Morgan, Lydekker, and Vail say that one sachem died on the voyage; Kalm, Ruttenber, and Foreman state that the fifth King died in England, Foreman adding that 'his name and burial place are not known'; and Drake suggests that the 'picture of the one that died was not probably taken'. For Colden's reference to 'five or six' Indians see above, p. 116.

John Oldmixon in his *History of England, During the Reigns of King William and Queen Mary, Queen Anne, King George I*, 1735, p. 452, in the course of one tortured sentence refers to 'four *Indian Casaques*' and 'five Monarchs'; Drake (see above) calls this 'his usual random mode of expression'. Six years later, in the second edition of his *British Empire in America*, i. 247, Oldmixon settled on five as the proper number, and, probably by misreading the account in Boyer's *Annals*, contributed the place-name Ganajohahare as the name of the fifth King. It is here appropriate to repeat that Oldmixon's 'reputation has survived that of his friend [Maynwaring] from the circumstance of his having given to the world the worst history of England that ever was or is ever likely to be written': Frederick William Wyon, *The History of Great Britain during the Reign of Queen Anne*, 1876, ii. 327.

The poisoning story may have a French source: see *Doc. Rel. N.Y.*, ix. 983.

For colonial records referring to four chieftains prior to sailing see, for example, the petition of Parker, the letter to Sunderland from Vetch and Dudley of 9 January 1710, and the appropriation of Massachusetts, quoted above, pp. 41, 42, and 43.

The legend of a King's demise in England or on the voyage possibly grew from the illness of one of the sachems in London or the death of Brant soon after their return home: see above, p. 3 and p. 40.

Pages 39–40. HENDRICK. The career of this famous Indian has been treated by Henry R. Schoolcraft, *Notes on the Iroquois*, Albany, 1847, pp. 415–16, and William L. Stone, *Life and Times of Sir William Johnson*, i. 549–51. Arthur C. Parker suggests that Hendrick may have been a Seneca: *An Analytical History of the Seneca Indians* (Researches and Transactions of the New York State Archaeological Association, vol. vi, pts. i-v), Rochester, 1926, opp. p. 96. For the suggestion to return to England after the death of Anne see George W. Schuyler, *Colonial New York*, ii. 56–57. For portraits of Hendrick other than those discussed later see R. W. G. Vail, *To Doctor R.*, pp. 223–5.

Hendrick was certainly a man of spirit and striking force. In

1713 Governor Hunter thought him 'a very turbulent subtle fellow, who since his return has given us more trouble than all the other Indians beside, and had he had the hundredth part of that power which was ascribed to him we must have been in actual war with them at this time', and proceeded to give an illustration of his troublesomeness: *C.S.P.*, *Amer.*, *1712–14*, p. 159. In 1744 Dr. Alexander Hamilton in his journal, *Itinerarium*, gave a particularly vivid account of Hendrick at an Indian conference as 'a bold, intrepid fellow': *Gentleman's Progress*, ed. Carl Bridenbaugh, Chapel Hill, 1948, pp. 112–13. See also above, p. 64.

In the collection of illustrations of historic matter on the Mohawk Valley made by Rufus Alexander Grider, now in the New York State Library, Albany, there is a drawing (album 6, page 8) of Hendrick's thigh bones as collected by one George Brown in 1862. The evidence of these bones (19½ inches in length) would make Hendrick a man of great size.

Dr. William N. Fenton of the Smithsonian Institution has kindly given his opinion that Hendrick's Indian name meant 'He holds the door open'.

Torax and Monelia as the son and daughter of Hendrick appear in *Ponteach: or the Savages of America*, by Major Robert Rogers, 1766, said to be the first American play to deal primarily with Indians.

Page 40. BRANT. Barclay, in a letter to the secretary of the S.P.G., 26 September 1710, stated that this sachem, 'one of the 4. Indians that were lately in England', had died two days before: 'A' MSS., vol. v, No. 176. Lydekker, *Faithful Mohawks*, p. 32, cites this reference. Brant's Indian name, again according to Dr. Fenton, would be translated as 'Old smoke' or 'Smoke that disappears'.

NICHOLAS. In 1734 the Rev. John Sergeant took to New Haven for schooling two lads—a lieutenant's son and 'Etowaukaum (who, by the way, is grandson by his mother to Etowaukaum, Chief of the River Indians, who was in England in Queen Anne's reign)': Samuel Hopkins, 'Historical Memoirs Relating to the Housatonic Indians (1693–1755)', *Magazine of History*, Extra No. 17, 1911, p. 29.

Pages 40–41. ARRIVAL AND STAY IN BOSTON. George W. Schuyler found an entry in the Bible of Abraham Schuyler—'1709. Dec 16ᵗʰ I went with Colo. Schuyler to England, and returned through the grace of God, July 26. 1710': *Colonial New York*, ii. 467. These dates would seem to refer to the departure from and arrival back home, i.e. New York, and as such they agree with other evidence. However, Schuyler, ii. 33, apparently used the first date to mean that the party sailed in December of 1709.

Samuel Mears is included among the 'Innholders in Boston in 1714', a list communicated by John S. H. Fogg, *New-England Historical and Genealogical Register*, xliii (1889), 59. For his bill see Massachusetts Archives, xxxi. 80–83. Material from these archives is quoted with the permission of Edward J. Cronin, Secretary of the Commonwealth of Massachusetts.

For Parker's petition of 5 June 1711, the resolution of the House of Representatives of the same date that he be allowed £10. 15*s*. 10*d*., and his bill (approved by Dudley 20 February 1710) for £13. 2*s*. 7*d*., see Massachusetts Archives, xxxi. 87, 88, and 89.

Pages 41–42. VETCH AND DUDLEY TO SUNDERLAND, 9 JANUARY 1710. Vetch Letter Book, pp. 113–14, quoted passage, p. 113.

Page 42. VETCH TO SUNDERLAND, 1 FEBRUARY. ibid., pp. 114–15, quoted passage, p. 114.

Two days before this letter Governor Saltonstall in a letter to Sir Henry Ashurst had carefully surveyed the 1709 affair: *Winthrop Papers, Collections of the Massachusetts Historical Society*, 6th ser., v (1892), 207–12.

Pages 42–43. VETCH AND DUDLEY TO SUNDERLAND, 3 FEBRUARY. Public Record Office, C.O. 5/9, No. 49, abstracted in *C.S.P., Amer., 1710–11*, p. 40. By misinterpreting this letter W. T. Morgan, *Mississippi Valley Historical Review*, xiii. 179, states that Schuyler and the chiefs sailed from Boston early in January 1710.

Captain Teate was not promptly repaid. On 10 August 1710 he sought the advice of Sunderland as to 'what method I should take to be reimbursed my Charges for bringing over the Indian Kings': Blenheim MSS., D. I. 32.

VETCH TO SUNDERLAND AND PRINGLE, 10 FEBRUARY. Vetch Letter Book, pp. 115–16, and Webster, *Samuel Vetch*, pp. 21–23, quoted passage, p. 22.

Page 43. GRANT OF MONEY TO SCHUYLER. Massachusetts Archives, xxxi. 62. Soon after arriving in England Schuyler petitioned for reimbursement of a large sum expended by him in furnishing the forts of Albany and Schenectady with firewood and also £300 'laid out in bringing to London the Four Indian Princes': *Acts of the Privy Council, Colonial Series, 1680–1720*, ii. 571.

Schuyler took with him the address and representation of New York by a resolution of 12 November: *Journal of the Votes and Proceedings of the General Assembly of the Colony of New-York . . . 1691–1743*, New York, 1764, i. 268–70.

VETCH TO LORD TREASURER. Undated, Vetch Letter Book, pp. 116–17, quoted passage, p. 117.

After the party had left Boston, Vetch perforce settled into the remainder of his winter of discontent and a spring of hope. By 15 May 1710 he had received not 'the least orders' for the renewal of the expedition: see his letter to Sunderland, *C.S.P., Amer., 1710–11*, p. 101. Here again he requests appointment to some vacant government.

Pages 43–44. DEPARTURE FROM BOSTON AND ARRIVAL IN ENGLAND. The *London Gazette* of 28–30 March contained a dispatch from Falmouth that on 24 March the *Severn-Inn Galley* arrived there from Boston in twenty-five days under convoy of the *Reserve*, from which it had been separated by bad weather. According to the *Dublin Intelligence*, 28 March, the *Reserve* put in at Kinsale. The *Daily Courant*, 4 April, reported that it passed by Plymouth to the east on 30 March, and the *Post Boy* and *Post-Man*, 1–4 April, recorded its arrival at Portsmouth on 2 April.

The most detailed account of the Kings' arrival is in the broadside *Royal Strangers Ramble*, 1710, which resorted to syncope:

> They no sooner approach'd
> P——h, but were Coach'd
>   In the G——rs old tatter'd Charriot.
> That drawn by two Nags,
> Seem'd ridden by Hags,
>   And disus'd to Fatigue, could not bear it.
> Tho' Sir J—, for their Sakes,
> Made 'em lean as two Rakes,
>   Jog down to the *Point* to receive 'em.

Freda F. Waldon, *Canadian Historical Review*, xvi (1935), 270, takes herefrom the port of arrival to be Plymouth. That Portsmouth is correct is shown not merely by the shipping news that the Kings' ship passed by Plymouth and put in at Portsmouth but also by the fact that 'Sir J—' fits Sir John Gibson, Lieutenant-Governor of the Portsmouth garrison, and does not fit the name of any Plymouth official: see John Chamberlayne's *Magnæ Britanniæ Notitia*, 1710, p. 561.

Page 44. RETURN TO BOSTON. See Boyer's *Annals*, ix. 191, and the *Diary of Samuel Sewall*, *Collections of the Massachusetts Historical Society*, 5th ser., vi (1879), 283. Cotton Mather on 22 May 1710 wrote to Samuel Penhallow: 'But, we may every day expect the *Dragon*, as a Forerunner, of Six Men of War, with a thousand Marines, of whom etc. Col. *Nicolson* is General, to pursue an Expedition, *first* against *Port-royal*. The Arrival of our Mast-fleet, and the Maqua's, may perhaps, a little retard, and alter, some of the Motions and Measures, but the thing will go on; and you will foresee that it is like to be a Summer of extreme Distress unto us.' *Collections of the Massachusetts Historical Society*, 7th ser., viii (1912), 35–36.

Schuyler's memorandum to Dudley is in the Massachusetts Archives, xxxi. 75.

For the sachems' letter to the Queen see *C.S.P., Amer., 1710–11*, p. 137. The letter to Archbishop Tenison, herein reproduced by permission of the Archbishop óf Canterbury and the Church Commissioners, is MS. 711.17 at the Lambeth Palace Library; there is a copy in the S.P.G. archives, 'A' MSS., vol. vi, No. 32. In *Notes and Queries*, 2nd ser., viii (1859), 454–5, S. R. M. quoted this letter, and referred thus to the totem signatures of tortoise, wolf, and bear: 'One of the latter is I think without doubt a tortoise; another, I imagine, was meant for a beaver; and the third, if not a horse, may be anything that could be made or mistaken for one.'

The sachems reached their homes about 26 July: see above, p. 119. William L. Stone, *Life and Times of Sir William Johnson*, i. 26, assigned the return of five chiefs to the autumn, and William Maitland, *History of London*, 1739, p. 325, said four Kings were 'nobly entertain'd at the Queen's Expence for divers Months in this City'.

Pages 44–46. GOVERNOR HUNTER. Robert Hunter had in 1707 been appointed Lieutenant-Governor of Virginia but, being captured by the French *en voyage* to America, never took office; he was exchanged for the Bishop of Quebec. His largest administrative problem in New York was the proper settlement of the Palatines. He has been identified as the Eboracensis of *Tatler* No. 69, whom Mr. Bickerstaff lauds without reserve.

For the Albany conference see *C.S.P., Amer., 1710–11*, pp. 490–500, quoted passages, pp. 490, 493, 494, 495, 499; cf. *Doc. Rel. N.Y.*,

v. 217–27. Hunter in October reported to Lord Dartmouth that the Indian Nations had given assurance of fidelity and desired missionaries and garrisons: *C.S.P., Amer., 1710–11*, pp. 228.

As to Mr. Bernardus Freeman, the Governor replied that he would promote his appointment but 'had not received the necessary orders relating to missionaries as yet from England which he expected dayly'. The Rev. Bernardus Freeman was the minister of the Dutch Reformed Church at Schenectady, and, though he administered to the Indians and translated holy words into their tongue, he would hardly be approved by the S.P.G. as their representative, a point perhaps overfine for savage eyes.

Anne Grant recounted that the sachems on their return to New York did not hasten home but at Albany summoned a congress of the elders of their own nation and the chiefs of their allies, and with bold, flowing eloquence persuaded their adherents to renounce all connexion with tribes under French influence and form a lasting league with 'the mighty people whose kindness had gratified, and whose power had astonished them, whose populous cities swarmed with arts and commerce, and in whose floating castles they had rode safely over the ocean'. See *Memoirs of an American Lady*, i. 31–32.

Pages 46–47. EXPEDITION OF 1710 AGAINST ACADIA. See Hutchinson, *History of Massachusetts-Bay*, ed. Mayo, ii. 134–7. For Nicholson's instructions, dated 18 March and 15 April, see the *Report and Collections of the Nova Scotia Historical Society for the Year 1878*, i (1879), 60–62, or the *Year-Book of the Society of Colonial Wars in . . . Massachusetts*, iii (1897), 82–84. The former annual also prints, pp. 63–104, the 'Journal of Colonel Nicholson at the Capture of Annapolis, 1710', which appeared in the *Boston News-Letter*, No. 342, 6 November 1710, now a great rarity, and as a sextuple issue probably the largest in the colonies up to that time. Hutchinson, ii. 134, noted the uncertainty of the Americans, when Nicholson arrived, on seeing the ships in the bay, the giving of the alarm, and the keeping of the militia under arms until evening. Hutchinson said, too, that Nicholson's ships 'seem to have lain there for orders, or until it should be made certain whether they were to be joined by any further force from England'; it is, however, not clear as to how much Nicholson knew of the potentialities of enlarging the campaign.

Vetch not infrequently in his letters seemed half-reconciled to the reduction of Port Royal in 1710, barring the success of the optimistic request for a total renewal of the Canada expedition; the quoted phrase appears in his letter to Ingoldsby, 31 October 1709, Vetch Letter Book, p. 101.

Nicholson and Vetch referred in a letter to Dartmouth, 16 September 1710, to the lack of directions sent the colonies before their arrival and their own consequent preparations: *C.S.P., Amer., 1710–11*, p. 215.

The proclamation by Dudley of a Thanksgiving for 16 November is given ibid., pp. 269–70.

Winston S. Churchill, *Marlborough: His Life and Times*, iv (1938), 384, stated that Commodore Martin after the capture of Nova Scotia in 1710 returned to London with the four chiefs.

Pages 47–49. EXPEDITION IN 1710 UNDER SHANNON. A large number of references to an American expedition and the five regiments in England by Godolphin and a smaller number by Marlborough appear in their correspondence, of which Archdeacon William Coxe made copies, now in the British Museum, from the Blenheim MSS. For the most important passages by Godolphin see B.M. MS. Add. 9108, ff. 172ᵛ, 186; 9109, ff. 15–15ᵛ, 67ᵛ–68, 150ᵛ–151, 160, 170–1, 181ᵛ–182. For passages by Marlborough see 9108, ff. 24, 26; 9109, ff. 155–155ᵛ; 9110, ff. 2–2ᵛ, 7–7ᵛ, 37; of these passages the first two have been printed by Coxe in his *Memoirs of . . . Marlborough*, 1819, iii. 179. Also in the letters to Marlborough from Henry Boyle, Secretary of State for the Northern Department, the progress of this expedition may be followed: see those of 23, 27 June, 11, 14, 21 July, 4, 18 August, and 19 September, Blenheim MSS., B. II. 1. On 17 April, three days before Godolphin first suggested to Marlborough renewing the large expedition, Sunderland apparently wrote Vetch that it was 'impossible to Spare such a number of forces as would be necessary for the Expedition against Canada': Public Record Office, C.O. 5/9, No. 50.

For Sunderland's directions to the Board of Ordnance, dated 17 and 25 May 1710, see State Papers Domestic, Anne, in the Public Record Office, S.P. 34/12, Nos. 72, 84; for the first of these see also B.M. MS. Add. 32694, f. 131, and Sunderland's Letter Book at Blenheim, ii. 452. Pertinent letters by Walpole at the War Office to Sunderland, 8 June, and to Dartmouth, 25 July, and from the Board of Ordnance to Dartmouth, 30 June, are in the same bundle of State Papers as above, Nos. 94, 147, 106. A letter by Pringle of 9 May, in Sunderland's Letter Book, vol. iii, shows that the Secretary of State desired a flying pacquet to reach Nicholson at Portsmouth; perhaps this undelivered express contained some word of plans for a force to follow.

For Shannon's commission and instructions see *C.S.P., Amer., 1710–11*, p. 134. Because the instructions were incompletely dated and unsealed, they were supposed not to have been given out: see B.M. MS. Add. 32694, ff. 132, 136.

For Dartmouth's letters to America see *C.S.P., Amer., 1710–11*, pp. 183–4, quoted passage, p. 184.

Jeremiah Dummer, the Massachusetts agent in London, on 6 July wrote Dartmouth that in obedience to his Lordship's commands he had again considered the question whether the season was too late to attempt anything against Canada and that he thought not, and a few days later wrote to request a place in the expedition: ibid., pp. 127–8, 133.

Thomas Hutchinson in his *History . . . of Massachusetts-Bay*, ed. Mayo, ii. 134, referred to advice received in New England that in July Lord Shannon lay under orders for sailing. Francis Parkman, *A Half-Century of Conflict*, 1892, i. 143, was obviously wrong in saying that 'towards midsummer, a strange spasm of martial energy seems to have seized the ministry'. Most historians do not allude at all to this proposed campaign, which left smaller archival and historiographical remains than it deserved.

Harley with the advent of the Hanoverians was accused of advising the Queen to consent to the disastrous, expensive expedition of 1711, although he 'well knew, that the said Project or Expedition having been frequently deliberated on and maturely considered, a short time before, in a Committee of Council, was then laid aside as dangerous and impracticable': *Articles of Impeachment of . . . Earl of Oxford*, 1727, p. 90. This is very likely a reference to the Shannon project, not to the 1709 enterprise as Hutchinson supposed, ii. 132.

Pages 49–53. EXPEDITION OF 1711. This enterprise, of the four expeditions prepared and the two sent, was much the most ambitious and has become the best known. It has gathered a considerable archive in *C.S.P., Amer., 1710–11* and *1711–12*, has been carefully described by Herbert L. Osgood in his chapter on the second inter-colonial war, *The American Colonies in the Eighteenth Century*, New York, 1924, and is usually at least noted in general histories. Among early colonial histories see especially Hutchinson's *History of . . . Massachusetts-Bay*, ed. Mayo, ii. 142–9, and Samuel Penhallow, *The History of the Wars of New-England, With the Eastern Indians*, Boston, 1726, pp. 62–67. Osgood rightly remarks, i. 67–68, the difficulties of conducting large operations—the difficulties of navigation, transportation, supply, communication, and health conditions—but it would seem that given good leadership this expedition of 1711 would most probably have succeeded. As to the four sachems, information sufficiently detailed is wanting to determine their personal participation in this expedition or in the enterprise of 1709.

For St. John's letters on the subject see his *Letters and Correspondence, Public and Private*, ed. Gilbert Parke, 1798, pp. 7, 12, 18, 30, 68–69, 142–3, 154–5, 161. For his letters to Harley see Historical Manuscripts Commission, *Fifteenth Report*, Part IV, *The Manuscripts of His Grace the Duke of Portland*, iv (1897), 652 and (quoted) 656. Some of the orders for the expedition are summarized in B.M. MS. Add. 32694, ff. 102ᵛ–104ᵛ. On 30 September 1710, only nine days after assuming the Secretaryship of State, St. John wrote the principal officers of Ordnance to provide cannon and powder for a Canadian expedition: State Papers Domestic, Anne, Public Record Office, S.P. 34/13, No. 64, and 44/109.

To carry on the design with all secrecy possible the ministry refrained from laying this expensive project before Parliament and also victualled the fleet so short that it had to take in fresh supplies at Boston: *The Allies and The Late Ministry Defended against France, And the Present Friends of France*, Part IV, 1712, pp. 36–37. The author of this tract, Francis Hare, strongly believed that no success could be hoped for from such expeditions. Stephen Martin-Leake in his *Life of Sir John Leake, Knt. Admiral of the Fleet*, 1750, p. 423, said of this 'ill concerted and worse executed' design that it 'was settled by Statesmen instead of Admirals, and kept a Secret from the only Persons that should have been privy to it'.

The arrival at Boston in July of 'three of the Sachems or Kings of the Five Indian nations of Iroquois our Allies' was noted by Colonel Richard King in his journal: *C.S.P., Amer., 1711–12*, p. 47. Their reception on the flagship was described by Admiral Walker in his *Journal: Or Full Account Of the late Expedition to Canada*, 1720, pp. 104–5. There is no indication that any of these sachems was one of the four Kings.

For Dudley's proclamation see his letter to St. John, 25 July: *C.S.P., Amer., 1711–12*, p. 38.

Saltonstall's letter to Harley, by then the Earl of Oxford, was written after and of course without knowledge of the disaster: Historical Manuscripts Commission, *Report on the Manuscripts of His Grace the Duke of Portland*, v (1899), 89.

For the gifts to Iroquois sachems at the conference of 25 August

1711 see *Doc. Rel. N.Y.*, v. 270. These pictures were presumably Simon's engravings of Verelst's portraits; there seems to be no record that the Kings knew any other product of their visit pictorial or belletristic discussed in Chapter III. For the fuller distribution of the pictures see Charles Burr Todd's 'Robert Hunter and the Settlement of the Palatines, 1710–1719', *The Memorial History of the City of New-York*, New York, ii (1892), 146, n., and *National Magazine*, xvii (1893), 305, n. For the gifts made at the conference of 3 October 1711 see *C.S.P., Amer., 1711–12*, p. 111.

The *Oxford Almanack for the Year of our Lord God MDCCXI* presented in the foreground the conventional classical and allegorical figures and in the right background the Royal Navy lying before a foreign town, a detachment of marines landed, and the General dispatched in a small boat. 'By these Figures we may understand there are great Designs form'd, the Knowledge of which are not yet blaz'd abroad, as has been practised upon former Occasions; but the Fleet is numerous, thereby representing, that the Security and Glory of *Britain* consists therein': *An Explanation of the Design of the Oxford Almanack For the Year 1711*, 1711, p. 22.

Page 56.   POPISH CATECHISM. *Present State of Europe*, xxi. 159. See also a dispatch of l'Hermitage to the States General, 23 May 1710, B.M. MS. Add. 17677DDD, ff. 498ᵛ–499; *A Compleat History of Europe* for 1710, p. 458; Jeremiah Dummer, *Letter to a Noble Lord on the Late Expedition to Canada*, 1712, p. 7; *Westminster Journal*, No. 323, 6 February 1748; and William Maitland, *History of London*, p. 325. The Society for the Propagation of the Gospel took cognizance of 'the Errors in the Quebec Catechism': Journal, i. 262, and *C.S.P., Amer., 1709–10*, p. 84. The responses in such a version of the French birth and English death of Christ do not, of course, appear in the *Catechisme du Diocese de Quebec*, by Jean de la Croix de Saint-Valier, Bishop of Quebec, Paris, 1702. A particularly interesting allusion to this story occurred in the appendix, on efforts made to Christianize the Indians, of Cotton Mather's *Bonifacius*, Boston, 1710, p. 198: 'At present, we can do nothing for those Bloody Salvages in the *Eastern Parts*, who have been taught by the *French Priests*, That the Virgin *Mary* was a *French* Lady, and that our Great Saviour was a *Frenchman*, and that the *English* murdered Him, and that He Rose from the Dead, & is taken up to the Heavens, but that all that would recommend themselves to His Favour, must Revenge His Quarrel on the English People; which issuing out from their Indiscoverable Swamps, they have often done with cruel Depredations.'

Pages 56–57. THOROUGHGOOD MOORE AND THOMAS BARCLAY. Humphreys, *Historical Account*, pp. 287–91, and Lydekker, *Faithful Mohawks*, pp. 18–24, quoted passage, p. 22.

Page 57. MEETINGS OF S.P.G., 1710. 19 May: S.P.G. Journal, i. 265–7; 16 June: i. 269–70; 21 July: i. 273–4; 18 August: i. 279; 15 September: i. 284–5.

Pages 57–58. MEETINGS OF S.P.G., 1711. 5 January: S.P.G. Journal, i. 334–5; 19 January: i. 337–40, quoted passages, p. 339; 1 February: i. 350–1, quoted passage, p. 351; 8 February: i. 352–3. For the sachems' letter from Boston of 21 July 1710, laid before the Board 5 January 1711, see above, p. 122. Barclay's letter, 26 September 1710, S.P.G. 'A' MSS., vol. v, No. 176, printed in *The Documentary History of the State of New-York*, ed. E. B. O'Callaghan, Albany, 4°, 1850, iii. 540–2, was read to the Society on 19 January 1711: Journal, i. 337–9. It also referred to the Indians' request for Freeman as missionary: see above, p. 46. For the letter of the Archbishop to the sachems, 21 March, see 'A' MSS., vol. vii, pp. 6*a*–7*a*; cf. Journal, ii. 2, 6, 10–11.

Pages 58–59. FORT, CHAPEL, AND PARSONAGE. Schuyler wrote on 30 December 1710 concerning the site of the establishment to a clergyman in England who had been kind to him there: Historical Manuscripts Commission, *Fifteenth Report*, Part IV, *The Manuscripts of His Grace the Duke of Portland*, iv (1897), 649–50. For the meeting of the Society, 22 June 1711, at which Nicholson presented a similar letter from Schuyler of 4 May, see the S.P.G. Journal, ii. 71.

For the conference with the Indians of 9 October 1711 see *Doc. Rel. N.Y.*, v. 278–9. The contract for the fort and chapel is reprinted in the same volume, pp. 279–81, and is quoted in part by Lydekker, p. 33, n. 1, who reproduced, pl. v, the plans designed by Col. John Redknap. The establishment in the Onondaga country was not built. In a letter of 25 May 1714 Andrews reported that the Onondaga sachems refused to have a fort built among them, and later, 17 October, that he understood no one would undertake to build it, 'this that is built being not paid for': S.P.G. 'A' MSS., vol. ix, p. 125, vol. x, p. 158.

The chasing away of the workmen is mentioned in a letter from New York by John Sharpe to the secretary of the S.P.G., 23 June 1712: 'A' MSS., vol. vii, p. 215.

Hunter recorded his garrisoning of the fort in a letter to the Council of Trade, 31 October 1712: *C.S.P., Amer., 1712–14*, p. 84.

The chapel was torn down to make way for the Erie Canal.

The missionary's house was not mentioned in the building contract or by Andrews as he began his mission; however, Barclay wrote to the S.P.G. in November 1711 that the fort would be finished the next July, that a house for the missionaries had likewise been ordered, and that carpenters were busy at work: 'A' MSS., vol. vii, p. 130; and (more important) the abstract of the year's work by the S.P.G. appended to the anniversary sermon preached by the Bishop of Ely, 1713, alludes to 'a Block-house at each corner, a Chappel and a Manse in the middle', p. 62. Referring to the present stone house, John J. Vrooman says, without documentation, that it was built in 1734: *Forts and Firesides of the Mohawk Country, New York*, Philadelphia, 1943, p. 102. Vrooman gives a photograph of the house, the second oldest in the Valley, opp. p. 101, as does W. Max Reid, *The Mohawk Valley: Its Legends and Its History*, New York, 1901, opp. p. 88.

Drawings of the fort, chapel, and present parsonage appear in the Grider Collection, New York State Library, Albany, album 2, pp. 8, 9, 27; album 3, pp. 27, 28.

Pages 59–60. PLATE AND FURNITURE. For these gifts see the annual report for 1712 appended to the anniversary sermon, preached by the Bishop of Ely, 1713, p. 62, quoted only in part by Lydekker, p. 31, and a letter from William Taylor, secretary of the Society, to Governor Hunter, 26 July 1712, S.P.G. 'A' MSS., vol. vii, p. 267. Cf. Reid, *Mohawk Valley*, pp. 87–88. For detail as to proper embroidery and the purple colour for this furniture see the warrant in the papers of the Lord Chamberlain's Department, Public Record Office, L.C. 5/155, p. 154. The estimate of the particulars of this warrant was approximately £255. 10*s*.: L.C. 5/71, No. 27.

The warrant, dated 10 April 1712, for the communion plate authorized that a set of three pieces, not exceeding the value of £60, be provided for each of the two Indian chapels, with the Queen's arms engraved and the gift properly superscribed, and delivered to Colonel Nicholson: Public Record Office, L.C. 5/109, p. 44, and 5/155, p. 155. The record, however, of the Jewel Office shows that two sets of six pieces each were delivered at a total charge of £140. 11*s*.: L.C. 9/47, p. 192.

After the American Revolution some of the Mohawks migrated to Canada with the silver, which was divided between the settlement at Grand River, Brantford, under Joseph Brant, and that at the Bay of Quinte. The Brantford group retained four pieces (photographs of which are reproduced by Lydekker, pl. iv, and by Reid, opp. p. 94) and was on exhibition in 1949 at the Royal Ontario Museum of Archaeology, Toronto. The Onondaga set went to St. Peter's Church, Albany, where it is encased in the War Memorial, a photograph of which has been reproduced on a picture postcard. It also appears as plate 14 in William M. Beauchamp's *A History of the New York Iroquois*, New York State Museum Bulletin 78, Albany, 1905.

Governor Hunter had brought Trinity Church, New York, a set of the plate in 1710: Morgan Dix, *A History of the Parish of Trinity Church in the City of New York*, New York, 1898, Part I, p. 179. A photograph is reproduced in a catalogue of the commemorative exhibition at the New-York Historical Society, in 1947, '250th Anniversary of the Parish of Trinity Church in the City of New York', p. 11. Christ Church, Boston, in a petition for the King's bounty of communion silver cited the precedent of the Mohawk set: Percival Merritt, 'The King's Gift to Christ Church, Boston, 1733', *Publications of the Colonial Society of Massachusetts*, xix (1918), 302.

Pages 60–64. ANDREWS AND THE S.P.G. Selection: S.P.G. Journal, 22 February 1712, ii. 173. At its meeting of 20 March the Society approved Andrews and directed him to wait upon the Archbishop for instructions: Journal, ii. 178. The next day the Archbishop wrote Lord Dartmouth that a missionary had been agreed on and that he had sent certain papers belonging to the whole matter by Nicholson, who was desirous to wait upon the Queen in order to perfect the affair and present wampum from the sachems: S.P.G. 'A' MSS., vol. vii, p. 9*a*. In a letter to Hunter of 27 March Dartmouth dealt succinctly, thanks to the memorandum just received from Nicholson, with the interest of the Queen in the Five Nations: *C.S.P., Amer., 1711–12*, pp. 252–3. For the letter by Archbishop Tenison, 29 May, to the sachems see B.M. MS. Stowe 119, f. 73, quoted by Edward Carpenter, *Thomas Tenison, Archbishop of Canterbury: His Life and Times*, 1948, p. 347.

Beginning of mission: Lydekker, p. 34, with the text, pp. 34–38, of most of Andrews' letter of 9 March 1713 to the Society from the 'A' MSS., vol. viii, pp. 143–7; and Barclay's letter to the S.P.G. of 17 December 1712, ibid., pp. 125–8, quoted passage concerning Hendrick's speech, p. 127. These letters were presented to the Board at its meeting of 9 October 1713: Journal, ii. 320–2. The meeting of the Commissioners of Indian Affairs in Albany, 15 November 1712, at which time Andrews began his ministry, is reported in the *Documentary History of the State of New-York*,

iii. 542–3. Concerning Hendrick's fear of the tithe see Governor Hunter's letter to the Council of Trade, 14 May 1713, *C.S.P.*, *Amer.*, *1712–14*, pp. 156–7, and *Doc. Rel. N.Y.*, v. 358.

Progress of mission: Lydekker, pp. 38–51, with excerpts from Andrews' letter of 1713–16, quoted passage, p. 39; and Humphreys, pp. 300–3. For the trip to the Oneida country see the letter by Andrews, 25 May 1714, not quoted by Lydekker, S.P.G. 'A' MSS., vol. ix, pp. 123–5, quoted passage, p. 125, and the list of baptized Indians, pp. 227–8. See also Humphreys, pp. 303–4.

End of mission: Lydekker, p. 51, and Humphreys, pp. 308–11, quoted passage, pp. 310–11.

Lydekker states, p. 33, that Andrews sailed for America on a ship called the *Four Kings*. For the missionary requested by the four Kings to go to their people on a ship so named would ask too much of coincidence, and in point of fact the letter cited as authority by Lydekker contains the name of no ship at all. However, letters between Andrews and the secretary of the Society (5 and 9 August 1712, S.P.G., 'A' MSS., vol. vii, pp. 31, 117) refer to his ship as the *Sorlings*, a name in script close enough to *Four Kings* for a wishful misreading.

Before Andrews received his appointment the Society read or heard celebration of its mode of increasing the Kingdom of God on Indian earth. At the anniversary meeting of 1711 William Fleetwood, Bishop of St. Asaph, preached the sermon without reference to the sachems; their visit instead was listed (p. 38) in the 'short Abstract of the most Material Proceedings and Occurrences in the Society' for the preceding year, added to the printed discourse. The annual sermon of 1712 was delivered by White Kennet, Dean of Peterborough and Chaplain in Ordinary to the Queen, on 'The Lets and Impediments in Planting and Propagating the Gospel of Christ', of which the first let was the 'affecting Conquest and usurping temporal Dominion, rather than enlarging the Kingdom of Christ' (p. 4) as Rome had done. The preacher claimed that progress in heathen lands had been made by proper alliance, purchase, and protection. 'It was a Sense of this just and Honourable Usage of them, that so lately brought over their Chiefs or Princes into this Nation, to do Honour unto our Queen, not by being made Vassals, but in becoming Friends and Confederates . . .' (p. 11).

Cotton Mather, referring to his new book *Bonifacius* in a letter to Sir William Ashurst of 9 November 1710, had objected to a passage in the S.P.G. anniversary sermon of 1706 by the Bishop of Chichester which reproached the colonies for having made no application to

conversion of the natives: 'It seems no Good must Ever be own'd
to be done, but what is done under ye Influence of the *mitre*. Lett
the Gentlemen of the New *Society* then be prevailed withal, to send
a Missionary or two, for the Christianizing of the *Iroquois* Indians,
whose princes (as they were fabulously called) appearing among
you, made so much noise the other day, on your side the water.
This would free your faithful and thoughtful Commissioners here,
from one of th^e most uneasy Sollicitudes; and the objects are without ye Bounds of New England.' *Some Correspondence between the
Governors and Treasurers of the New England Company in London and the
Commissioners of the United Colonies in America,* ed. John W. Ford,
1896, p. 91.

An interesting product of the Andrews mission was the publication by William Bradford at New York in 1715 of the first Book of
Common Prayer printed in America, *The Morning and Evening Prayer,*
translated by Andrews' interpreter Lawrence Claesse 'into the
Mahaque Indian Language'. It included the Litany, Church Catechism,
family prayers, and several chapters of the Old and New Testaments.
The title-pages and headings were in English and Mohawk; the text
was in Mohawk. Claesse had long acted in New York as Indian
interpreter; the officers at Wood Creek (see above, p. 32) recommended him to go to England with the sachems, but Colonel
Schuyler preferred his own cousin, whose better command of
English would doubtless offset a lesser knowledge of Mohawk. See
Humphreys, pp. 302–3: *Doc. Rel. N.Y.*, viii. 815–16; James Constan-
tine Pilling, *Bibliography of the Iroquois Languages,* Bureau of Ethno-
logy, Smithsonian Institution, Bulletin No. 6, Washington, 1888,
pp. 44–45.

Pages 64–65. PILGRIM BOTANIST. For the letter from More to Sherard, 27 October 1722, see the Sherard Correspondence, iv. 561, in the
library of the Royal Society. For Sherard's letter to Richardson, 18
January 1724, see John Nichols, *Illustrations of the Literary History
of the Eighteenth Century,* 1817, i. 391–2.

NOTES TO CHAPTER III

Pages 66–67. JOHN VERELST. The best study of the iconography of
the Kings is R. W. G. Vail's 'Portraits of "The Four Kings of
Canada"', a Bibliographical Footnote', in *To Doctor R.*, a very
privately printed volume of essays honouring A. S. W. Rosenbach,
Philadelphia, 1946, pp. 218–26.

For payment to Verelst of £100 and the added fee of £7. 10*s*. see the warrant, signed by Shrewsbury and dated 30 September 1710, in the Lord Chamberlain's Department, Miscellanea, Public Record Office, L.C. 5/155, p. 36. The reference by Zacharias Conrad von Uffenbach in his *Travels* may be found in the translation by W. H. Quarrell and Margaret Mare, *London in 1710*, 1934, p. 157. According to a manuscript note in the British Museum copy, of *A Catalogue of Pictures . . . the Collection of Mr. John Verelst, Painter*, [1728], p. 2, on 9 May were sold for £1. 14*s*. 'Four half lengths of the Indian Kings, by Verelst'. These were probably the artist's drafts and the basis for the whole lengths with backgrounds. The present location of neither the half-lengths nor the whole-lengths is apparently known.

For references to the *True Effiges* see the *Supplement*, No. 364, 12–15 May 1710, and *Tatler*, No. 172, 13–16 May. A reproduction of this print, which is not included in Vail's survey, appeared in Alwin Thaler's *Shakspere to Sheridan*, Cambridge, Mass., 1922, opp. p. 279, from a copy in the Harvard Theatre Collection.

The engravings by Simon were advertised in the *Tatler*, November and December 1710, Nos. 250, 253, 256, 261, and 267; the last announcement specified seven shops where the prints could be had. These advertisements also placed the originals by Verelst at Kensington Palace. Simon's engravings, herein reproduced from copies in the New York Public Library, have been described by John Chaloner Smith, *British Mezzotinto Portraits*, 1883, iii. 1095–6, and reprinted by J. R. Bartlett, 'The Four Kings of Canada', *Magazine of American History*, ii (1878), opp. p. 152; Justin Winsor, *Narrative and Critical History of America*, opp. p. 107; Francis Parkman, *A Half-Century of Conflict*, Boston, 1907, opp. pp. 146, 148; Charles Burr Todd, 'Robert Hunter and the Settlement of the Palatines, 1710–1719', *Memorial History of the City of New-York*, ii. 142–5, and *National Magazine*, xvii (1893), 304, 306–8; and Samuel Adams Drake, *The Border Wars of New England*, New York, 1897, pp. 252–5. Clark Wissler, *Indians of the United States*, New York, 1940, opp. p. 112, includes the engraving of Brant; Katherine Schuyler Baxter, *A Godchild of Washington*, London and New York, 1897, p. 341, and Arthur C. Parker, *Analytical History of the Seneca Indians*, opp. p. 96, reprint that of Hendrick; Vail, opp. pp. 218, 219, gives the pictures of Brant and Hendrick; and Francis Whiting Halsey, *Old New York Frontier*, opp. p. 158, reproduces those of Brant, Hendrick, and Nicholas.

Page 68. BERNARD LENS. In the Department of Prints and Drawings of the British Museum are the two sets of miniatures, one of three portraits and one of four, which are smaller. Neither seems obviously to have been a draft for the other. Also in the British Museum (MS. Add. 5253, ff. 19–22) are water-colour versions of the Lens portraits in full length with the costumes completed by conventional black small-clothes and stockings and shoes; these pictures seem closer to the set of three miniatures.

A note on No. 50 in the 1789 edition of the *Spectator* remarked that the miniatures were inscribed upon the back 'Drawn *by* the life, May 2, 1710, by Bernard Lens, *Jun.*' See also Bartlett, *Magazine of American History*, ii. 155. The miniatures are now so mounted that any such inscription is obscured.

The engraving here reproduced as a frontispiece is in the New York Public Library. For descriptions see J. C. Smith, *British Mezzotinto Portraits*, iv. 1692–3, and Vail, *To Doctor R.*, pp. 221–2. The Lens Kings have been reproduced by the autotype process from engravings in Smith's own collection, as the fifth in *Twelve Portraits of Persons Connected During the Last Century with the States of America (Chiefly in Their Colonial Period)*, 1884.

Page 68. JOHN FABER. The engravings of the portraits by Faber have been reproduced in the *125th Annual Report* of the New York State Library, Albany, 1942, opp. pp. 48, 49, and described by J. C. Smith, *British Mezzotinto Portraits*, i. 288, and Vail, *To Doctor R.*, p. 222. Vail also discusses, pp. 222–3, the copies by Schenck. The engraving of Hendrick herein reproduced is from the Ayer Collection in the Newberry Library.

Pages 68–69. THE FOUR INDIAN KINGS SPEECH. This rare sheet, combining pictures and verse, is not cited in the bibliographical articles by Vail and by Waldon (see below). A copy with the colophon inked out is in the British Museum. A photograph of this British Museum print is reproduced in *Some Indian Events of New England*, by Allan Forbes, Boston, 1914, p. 28.

Page 70. THE ROYAL STRANGERS RAMBLE. What may be the sole surviving copy of this ballad is in the collection of the Earl of Crawford, and is listed in *Bibliotheca Lindesiana: Catalogue of a Collection of English Ballads of the XVIIth and XVIIIth Centuries*, Aberdeen, 1890, p. 146. For other passages see above, pp. 10, 44, 121.

Pages 70–73. THE FOUR INDIAN KINGS. The text here followed is that of the folio sheet with no imprint and two cuts, one of three conventional kings and one of a lady. It is in the Harvard College Library, as is a copy with cut of three kings and a star. The most complete list of printings of this ballad may be found in Freda F. Waldon's 'Queen Anne and "The Four Kings of Canada", a Bibliography of Contemporary Sources', *Canadian Historical Review*, xvi (1935), 266–75. Miss Waldon, in her list of the nine printings of the shorter version, does not include one by Turner in Coventry, with cut of four kings, and one 'Printed and Sold at No. 4, Aldesmary Church Yard', with cut of three kings; both of these folio sheets, five columns, are in the Harvard College Library. There were probably still other printings of this popular ballad.

This poem has been given more recent circulation by Bartlett, *Magazine of American History*, ii. 153–5; *An American Garland: Being a Collection of Ballads Relating to America, 1563–1759*, ed. C. H. Firth, Oxford, 1915, pp. 60–68; and Bissell, *American Indian in English Literature of the Eighteenth Century*, pp. 215–19.

Pages 73–74. ELKANAH SETTLE. *A Pindaric Poem, on the Propagation of the Gospel in Foreign Parts. A Work of Piety So Zealously Recommended and Promoted By Her Most Gracious Majesty*, 1711, pp. iii–iv, 13.

Pages 74–75. ALEXANDER POPE. *Windsor-Forest*, 1713, pp. 16–17. Of course, Pope's 'Kings shall sue' may be a reference to European monarchs. Charles Kenneth Eves, *Matthew Prior, Poet and Diplomatist*, New York, 1939, p. 221, has suggested that at the time of the Indians' visit the young Pope 'conceived the idea of writing some "American Pastorals" '.

Pages 75–77. DANIEL DEFOE. For the first allusion see the *Review*, vol. vii, No. 61, 15 August 1710, and for the passage on the Mohocks, vol. viii, No. 153, 15 March 1712. There is a passing reference to the Kings in vol. viii, No. 196, 24 June.

MOHOCKS. For the society of Mohocks see Robert J. Allen, *The Clubs of Augustan London*, Cambridge, Mass., 1933, pp. 106–18. The quoted phrase and couplet on the Mohocks are from John Gay's *Trivia*, iii. 322, 325–6. Besides *Spectator* No. 324, the Mohocks are alluded to or treated in Nos. 323, 332, 335 (on Sir Roger's fear of falling into their hands), and 347. A half-sheet of 1712, *The Town-Rakes: Or, The Frolicks of the Mohocks or Hawkubites*, makes no allusion to the Indians. Another, *An Argument Proving from History, Reason, and Scripture, That the Present Mohocks and Hawkubites are the Gog and Magog mention'd in the Revelations* . . ., says that there will be a day when the Mohocks 'shall come from the furthermost Part of *America*, yea, from the furthermost Corner of the furthermost Part of the Earth'.

Pages 77–78. TRACTS OF 1710. In *The History and Progress of the four Indian Kings*, printed for A. Hinde, the quoted passage is on p. 3. George F. Horner has recognized a close resemblance, even a verbatim correspondence, between this passage and one in John Lawson's *History of Carolina*. An examination of the early publishing history of Lawson's work shows that it first appeared as the April and May 1709 issues of *A New Collection of Voyages and Travels*, and that the same setting of type was used for the separate publication, *A New Voyage to Carolina*, 1709, with the passage in question on page 29. Apparently the anonymous author of the *History and Progress* lifted for his tract on the Iroquois a passage from Lawson's lengthy treatment of the Southern Indians. Since Lawson was not in England during 1710 after the visit of the Kings, there was no opportunity for him to write the tract himself and insert a favourite passage of his own for double duty.

The History of the Four Indian Kings was printed and sold by Edward Midwinter.

The Four Kings of Canada, printed and sold by John Baker, was reprinted in facsimile by J. E. Garratt & Co. in London, 1891. This tract is quoted above, pp. 2–3, 97.

A political pamphleteer would know the value of the Kings for current allusion. One such reference occurs in *Dick and Tom: a Dialogue about Addresses*, 1710, p. 6, where Tom is ridiculing the addresses brought in from all parts of the country (about the time of the Sacheverell trial) to offer the lives and fortunes of the signers to the Queen: 'And suppose one of the *Indian* Kings, who was here t'other day, should have told us, that it was a solemn Custom in his Country for his Subjects to take an opportunity to offer him their Lives and Estates, when he stood in no need of either; yet by the Custom of his Country, that he must stand and hear all their Stories, of which he can believe very little: should not we think that he had been King of *Ganderland*?'

The lively pamphlet, *A True and Faithful Account of the Last Distemper and Death of Tom. Whigg, Esq*: Part I, 1710, pp. 32–33, deposed the Kings into a symbol of anti-monarchy. 'To promote the same Design of introducing a Commonwealth, you have made use, say they, of a great many crafty Devices colour'd over with Pretences of doing Honour to the State; as particularly, the bringing over hither four unknown Persons, *Psalmanaazars* I suppose, from the *West-Indies*, under the notion of Kings and Emperors, exposing 'em about the Town all four in a Hackney-Coach, from Tavern to Tavern, and treating them, and lodging them I suppose four in a Bed, with no other reasonable Design but that of lessening the Honour due to the Majesty of Kings, and rendring them little and contemptible in the Eyes of the Populace: all this while forgetting the Illustrious House of *Hannover*—.' The importation of the Indians, actually, had been initiated by colonial leaders, not the Whig ministry.

Another pamphlet, *The Indian's Petition: or, Black Jack's Pawawing to Don Pluto, Lord of the Dark Regions. Done from his Spanish Notes* 'By Adam Addlestaff, Gent. Near Kinsman to the Bickerstaffs,' despite such a promising title seems to have no connexion with the Kings and practically none with Indians, but to bid for sales by a pointless attachment to a current popular topic.

Pages 78–81.   *TATLER.* This text of No. 171 is that of the original folio sheet. Cadaroque is Cataraqui, on Lake Ontario, renamed Fort Frontenac and now Kingston.

The upholsterer of King Street, whom the sachems could honour so graciously for his goodness as host and skill with furniture, was without doubt the counterpart of the Thomas Arne of the 'Two Crowns and Cushions' who had been engaged to lodge them. Other *Tatlers*, however, in April and May (Nos. 155, 160, 178) dealt with an upholsterer whose avocation as newsmonger offered occasion for satire on the press and its enthusiasts. These several essays in close neighbourhood create an easy confusion between these two men of the same trade. But their characters and circumstances were so different that the Kings' upholsterer and the political upholsterer would seem certainly to have had different originals if, indeed, the latter had a likeness in life. It becomes, albeit, rather a pity to distinguish between our upholsterers, for when the political newsmonger awakens Mr. Bickerstaff before dawn of 17 April to talk with him 'about a Piece of Home-News, that every Body in Town will be full of Two Hours hence', the reader is tempted to imagine these are tidings that four Indian princes from America had been bedded at his home within the hour or would arrive in King Street before noon. Such a coincidence is uncommonly pretty, but the sacrifice of the actual to the appropriate here, as so often, would be a mischief which even capricious History could not approve.

Morphew's continued *Tatler*, 18 January 1711, mentioned the Kings.

Pages 81–85. SPECTATOR. This text of No. 50 and that of No. 56 are from the original folio sheets. The phrase 'as smooth as polished Marble' was altered to 'as smooth as the Surface of a Pebble' in the first collected edition, 1712, and 'who were the Men of the greatest Perfections in their Country' became 'who were the Persons of the greatest Abilities among them'. Was the first of these two changes the result of the letter from J. H. (above, p. 86)?

The notion that St. Paul's was erected by scooping out a great rock had, of course, come from no experience in American architecture. Addison had taken the idea from his reading and applied it to the Cathedral, which during the year of the Indian visit received the topmost stone of the lantern in its reconstruction after the Great Fire. The conception of the painsome hollowing of a large rock into a church had appeared as that of a rustic North Briton in a book by Martin Martin, *A Description of the Western Islands of Scotland*, 1703, pp. 297–8. An inhabitant of St. Kilda, on being asked his opinion of the high church at Glasgow, answered 'that it was a large Rock, yet there were some in *St. Kilda* much higher, but that these were the best Caves he ever saw; for that was the Idea which he conceiv'd of the Pillars and Arches upon which the Church stands'. This passage, be it added, so 'particularly struck' Michael Johnson, bookseller of Lichfield, that he directed to it the attention of his son Samuel: *Boswell's Life of Johnson*, ed. G. B. Hill, rev. L. F. Powell, Oxford, 1934, i. 450.

In the use of an Indian come to London, Tom Brown, *Amusements Serious and Comical*, 1700, anticipated Addison's satiric method: see Hamilton Jewett Smith, *Oliver Goldsmith's The Citizen of the World*, New Haven, 1926, p. 137, and Benjamin Boyce, *Tom Brown of Facetious Memory*, Cambridge, Mass., 1939, p. 137 n. Addison again used the device of the foreign observer in the letter from the Ambassador of Bantam to his royal master in the *Spectator* essay for 21 June 1714, No. 557, on the nonsense and hypocrisy of polite conversation.

In *Spectator* No. 11 Steele's Arietta had retold the moving story of Inkle and Yarico from the work of the Barbadoes traveller Richard Ligon. For the large popularity of this tale as a theme in England, France, and Germany see Lawrence Marsden Price, *Inkle and Yarico*

Album, Berkeley, 1937. Was Steele's interest in this Indian history the result of his interest in the Kings and essay on them in the *Tatler* the year before?

Gilbert Chinard in the introduction to his edition of the Baron de Lahontan's *Dialogues* and *Mémoires*, Baltimore, 1931, p. 59, suggests that the *Tatler* essay by Steele and the *Spectator* paper by Addison may owe something to Lahontan. Edward Chauncey Baldwin, 'La Bruyère's Influence upon Addison', *Publications of the Modern Language Association of America*, xix (1904), 489, on the basis of a very slight resemblance between a part of the *Spectator* paper and a passage in the *Caractères* concludes 'that Addison probably owed more in the way of suggestion to La Bruyère than to Swift'.

A letter to the *Spectator* in the *Plain Dealer*, No. 7, 24 May 1712, began thus: 'I would by no means be thought to write to you out of any disrespect, either to your Person, or Merit; I could wish every one of your *Spectators* were as valuable, as those upon the Humours of Sir *Roger*, or the Observations of the *Indian Kings*.' Reprinted in the *Miscellaneous Works of Dr. William Wagstaffe*, 2nd ed., 1726, p. 249.

Steele's *Tatler* paper and Addison's *Spectator* essay have properly been cited as early literary specimens of primitivism. See Hoxie Neale Fairchild, *The Noble Savage: a Study in Romantic Naturalism*, New York, 1928, pp. 42-45, and Margaret M. Fitzgerald, *First Follow Nature: Primitivism in English Poetry, 1725-1750*, New York, 1947, p. 30. Steele, to be sure, shows through his character Timoleon some interest in the virtues of generous gratitude and natural justice, but the latter part of his essay becomes a satire on the doubting, contradicting Minucius. Addison seems less concerned with praise of the primitive than reproof of English irreligion, party warfare, and social foibles through the device of the foreign observer whose apparently 'wild Remarks' contain 'something very reasonable.' Both essays comment on the guilt of the 'narrow Way of Thinking' which calls barbarous such men and manners as are strange, and both are written from a journalistic interest in the 'new or uncommon'. Many of the high placed and low in London must have given attention to the novel spectacle of these outlanders with no larger consideration for noble savagery or the last enchantments of the Golden Age than for the catch of current colour or the related matters of war, gospel, and commerce.

Pages 85–86. JONATHAN SWIFT. *Journal to Stella*, ed. Harold Williams, Oxford, 1948, i. 254-5. For the reference to '*A Voyage into*

England' see *A Tale of a Tub*, ed. A. C. Guthkelch and D. Nichol
Smith, Oxford, 1920, pp. 2, 345–6.

In his annotated, interleaved copy of the *Spectator* (Henry W. and
Albert A. Berg Collection, New York Public Library) Weeden
Butler cited John Nichols on Swift's relation to the periodical and
added, opposite No. 50, his own opinion: 'But it would perhaps,
puzzle us both, to assign a good Reason, for Swift's original *Communication*; his subsequent *Taciturnity*; and his final *Chit Chat of
Information* to *the Lady*. There was nothing for him to be ashamed
of in this Nº. L of the Spectator. I wish it were *the worst of his Works*.
But, when a Man has *given* his Purse, his Book, or his Mind, tis no
longer *his own*. It is a sufficient Compliment to even a Swift, that
an *Addison* found the Egg; & thus pleasingly hatched, what the
ostrich Parent threw out at Random; and perhaps never more
thought of, till it appeared in full Plumage as on the opposite Page.'

Albert Matthews, *Notes and Queries*, clxxvi (1939), 410–11, has
identified the four sachems with the 'Iroquois Virtuosi' of the
introduction to Swift's *Discourse concerning the Mechanical Operation
of the Spirit*, 1710.

Pages 86–87. LETTER TO THE *SPECTATOR*. This letter by J. H.
appeared in *Original and Genuine Letters sent to the Tatler and Spectator,
During the Time those Works were publishing*, 1725, i. 258–60. These
two volumes of letters, 'None of which have been before Printed',
were with Steele's permission collected by and published for Charles
Lillie, perfumer, who had been associated with Steele and Addison.
Was J. H. one John Henley, who is credited with the humorous
letters on punning and physiognomy in the *Spectator*, Nos. 396 and
518?

Page 88. *ROYAL REMARKS*. Several allusions in this shilling tract,
printed without date or name of publisher, point to 1730 as the
probable year of composition.

Pages 88–89. *UNIVERSAL SPECTATOR*. The two essays, appearing in
Nos. 695–6, 30 January and 6 February 1742, were reprinted in
the February issue of the *London Magazine*, xi. 83–86, and of the
Scots Magazine, iv. 73–76.

Pages 89–90. *ST. JAMES'S CHRONICLE*. No. 214, 21–24 July 1762. In
Nos. 211 and 212 the letter from the Cherokee King was mentioned
as an imminent publication.

Page 90. PUBLICATIONS. One type of publication the Kings failed to attract was the pictorial playing-card. In the late seventeenth century and the early eighteenth it was the practice to print packs of geographical and historical cards illustrating current events or interests. Two sets had been issued with the club suit given to America; decks were sold portraying the Popish Plot, Monmouth's Rebellion, the reign of James II, the Revolution, Marlborough's victories, the reign of Anne, and even the impeachment of Dr. Sacheverell. Though the American chiefs were often presented by engraver and printer, they did not appear on a mere deck of cards when at the only time in English history a manufacturer had the whole Western world for embellishment and precisely four Kings ready at hand.

INDEX